THE ELECTRONIC SCHOOLHOUSE:

The IBM Secondary School Computer Education Program

THE ELECTRONIC SCHOOLHOUSE:

The IBM Secondary School Computer Education Program

Hugh F. Cline
Randy Elliot Bennett
Roger C. Kershaw
Martin B. Schneiderman
Brian Stecher
Susan Wilson

Educational Testing Service

LEA LAWRENCE ERLBAUM ASSOCIATES, PUBLISHERS
1986   Hillsdale, New Jersey   London

Copyright © 1986 by Lawrence Erlbaum Associates, Inc.
All rights reserved. No part of this book may be reproduced in
any form, by photostat, microform, retrieval system, or any other
means, without the prior permission of the publisher.

Lawrence Erlbaum Associates, Inc., Publishers
365 Broadway
Hillsdale, New Jersey 07642

Library of Congress Cataloging in Publication Data
Main entry under title:

The Electronic Schoolhouse: The IBM Secondary School
Computer Education Program

   Bibliography: p.
   Includes index.
   1. IBM microcomputers. 2. Electronic data processing
—Study and teaching (Secondary) 3. Computer-assisted
instruction. I. Cline, Hugh F.
QA76.8.I1015E47   1986   373.13'9445   85-13086
ISBN 0-89859-649-1
ISBN 0-89859-795-1 (pbk)

Printed in the United States of America
10 9 8 7 6 5 4 3 2 1

Contents

Foreword ix
Preface xi

Chapter 1 **BACKGROUND AND DESIGN OF THE PROGRAM**
Hugh F. Cline 1

  Background *1*
  Program Design *4*
  Program Goals *7*

Chapter 2 **SELECTION OF PROGRAM PARTICIPANTS**
Hugh F. Cline 9

  TTI Selection *9*
  Secondary School Selection *14*
  Statistical Summary *23*
  Summary *25*

Chapter 3 **HARDWARE AND SOFTWARE SELECTION**
Roger C. Kershaw 27

  Hardware Selection *27*
  Software Selection *31*
  Summary *37*

Chapter 4	**STAFF TRAINING** *Martin B. Schneiderman* and *Brian Stecher*	39
	Training the Teacher-Trainers *40* Training the Teachers *46* Common Characteristics of the Best Summer Institutes *56* Summary *61*	
Chapter 5	**NETWORK SUPPORT AND PROGRAM OPERATIONS** *Randy Elliot Bennett*	63
	ETS Network Support *63* TTI Network Support *81* IBM Network Support *83* Summary *84*	
Chapter 6	**THE COST OF IMPLEMENTING COMPUTER-BASED EDUCATION** *Brian Stecher*	87

	An Illustrative Dialogue *88*
	Cost Analysis Procedures *89*
	Distribution of Costs/Resources in
	    IBM Program Schools *91*
	Aggregated Costs *99*
	Comparison with Preliminary Cost
	    Projections *101*
	Discussion *101*
	Sources of Funds for Computer-Based
	    Education *106*
	A Final Note: Is Computer Education
	    Worth the Cost? *108*
	Summary *109*	

Chapter 7	**PROGRAM IMPACT** *Randy Elliot Bennett* and *Susan Wilson*	111
	Goal Attainment *111* Related Effects *120* Consumer Reaction *124* Summary *128*	

| Chapter 8 | **SUMMARY AND RECOMMENDATIONS**
Hugh F. Cline and *Martin B. Schneiderman* | 129 |

            Significance of the Program   *129*
            Recommendations   *132*
            Summary   *139*

Epilogue   141

APPENDIX A: Microcomputer Laboratory Design and Usage Suggestions   143

APPENDIX B: Publications about the IBM Secondary School Computer Education Program   147

References   149

Author Index   151

Subject Index   153

Foreword

Something new and potentially very significant educationally is happening in schools across the nation. The computer is entering the school and classroom in growing numbers. The costs of computers are coming within the reach of most schools across the country and this access is likely to grow. In fact, there is evidence that the education sector is one of the fastest growing consumers of computers.

The potential benefits of this rapid introduction of technology in the nation's schools are tremendous. Teaching and learning activities can be supplemented and strengthened, instruction could be highly individualized, those in need of extra help can be more effectively served, and teachers can be substantially aided with their instructional and administrative responsibilities. New approaches to instruction, such as student participation in simulations, could become commonplace in the classroom.

In the rush to embrace computers for educational purposes, it is important to understand the importance of careful planning and preparation. Personal computers in the 1980s are in educational vogue; schools must act with care so that they are not remembered as a fad by the 1990s.

The keynote to success for computer education programs is instructional planning and teacher preparation. This book describes a program that used a thoughtful and planned approach to the introduction and integration of computing into the secondary school curriculum. While making quality computers and computer programs available, the IBM Secondary School Computer Education Program also provided substantial teacher training and followup educational and technical support. Furthermore, by promoting the use of the personal computers in many different subject areas, the program produced more widespread and equitable student access. I believe the IBM Secondary School Computer Education Program is a pioneering step in the development of educational computing in secondary education and hope that this book serves to help others benefit from the experience gained in this important collaborative endeavor between business and the schools.

Gregory R. Anrig
President
Educational Testing Service

Preface

This book documents the IBM Secondary School Computer Education Program. We, the authors, helped design and administer the program under a contract between IBM and Educational Testing Service (ETS). The expected audience for the book includes federal and state education officials, university and college teacher-training faculty, school district superintendents and their staffs, public and private school administrators, teachers, students, and parents—in sum, all those concerned with the current status and future of secondary education in the United States.

Chapter 1 describes the origins and design of the program. Chapter 2 describes the rationale for and the procedures employed in selecting the teacher training institutes and the secondary schools that participated in the program. This chapter also includes descriptive statistics on the schools. Chapter 3 describes the hardware and software components of the program and presents an account of the pedagogical perspectives and assumptions used in making these selections. Chapter 3 also discusses the problems of maintenance and security of the donated items.

Chapter 4 reviews the various levels of training that took place in the program, focusing upon the instruction provided to the teacher trainers and to the school faculty. Network services, as provided by the staffs of the teacher-training institutes, ETS, and IBM are described in chapter 5. This chapter also includes descriptions of the program operations from the perspective gained in implementing the network support services. Because the question of financing the use of computers in schools is of paramount importance, we have devoted all of chapter 6 to an analysis of the direct and indirect costs incurred by participating schools.

At several points during the program, we collected data from the schools describing the nature and extent of computer education activities. In chapter 7 we present the results of our analyses of these data. Finally, chapter 8 summarizes the volume and makes specific recommendations that will enable educators to learn from our experiences so that they can promote effective use of computers in other schools.

We wish to acknowledge the support and contributions of the many organizations and individuals who made this program possible. First and foremost is the unprecedented and magnanimous support of the IBM Corporation. Dr. Michael deV. Roberts, Program Officer at IBM, ably gave direction with his untiring energy and commitment. In addition, the following corporations made substantial contributions: Alpha Software, Computer Access, Cybertronics International, Hayes Microcomputer Products, Koala Technology, McGraw-Hill Book Company, Science Research Associates, Software Publishing, Source Telecomputing, and Tymnet. The following software firms made substantial discounts available to program participants: Lotus, Micropro, Microsoft, Visicorp, and Volkswriter.

Within ETS we acknowledge the invaluable program contributions of Thomas Barrows, Program Manager, Senior Research Assistants Roberta Klein and Michaele Mikovsky, Professor Kenneth Sipser, on sabbatical leave from the State University of New York at Oswego, the training contributions of William Nemceff, the technical assistance of Douglas Forer and Eric Holme, the fiscal management assistance of Eugene Horkay, the editorial assistance of Elsa Rosenthal, and the administrative and secretarial assistance of Lois Barrett, Corrine Cohen, Altamese Sherrell, Beverly White, and Virginia Wilson.

Finally, we express our deep appreciation to all the teacher-training institute staff, school principals, teachers, and students who so enthusiastically embraced and conducted this program. We particularly acknowledge the outstanding contributions of Professors Terry Cannings and John McManus of Pepperdine University.

Hugh F. Cline
Randy Elliot Bennett
Roger C. Kershaw
Martin B. Scheiderman
Brian Stecher
Susan Wilson

1 Background and Design of the Program

Hugh F. Cline

BACKGROUND

In the spring of 1983, IBM Corporation initiated an $8 million computer education program to develop and refine a model for the effective use of computers in secondary schools. The program established and coordinated a three-state network of 12 teacher-training institutes and 89 high schools representing a cross section of the nation's schools. Educational Testing Service (ETS) was contracted to assist in the design and administration of this landmark program.

The donation to each school consisted of laboratories of 15 IBM Personal Computers (PCs) and extensive sets of software for word processing, database management, graphics, electronic spreadsheets, tutorials, learning games, and programming languages. In addition, the schools were provided with telecommunications equipment that permitted students, teachers, and teacher trainers to communicate by electronic mail. This program made possible for high school students and teachers, the most extensive use to date of microcomputers, telecommunications, and commercially available applications software.

The events, trends, and activities that contributed to establishing the IBM Secondary School Computer Education Program were multiple and interrelated. As this program came into being early in 1983, three general factors were important background conditions. First was an emerging public consensus that the nation's schools were in dire need of substantial remedial efforts; second was the phenomenal market success experienced by several microcomputer manufacturers; and third was increasing pressure to create private/public collaborations aimed at improving the quality of education. We briefly describe these factors and indicate how they contributed to the creation, design, and implementation of the IBM Program.

During 1983 a plethora of critical commission, task force, and study reports appeared (Boyer, 1983; National Commission on Excellence in Education, 1983; Task Force on Education for Economic Growth, 1983; Twentieth Century Fund Task Force on Federal Elementary and Secondary Education Policy, 1983). Each report in its own way denounced the exceptionally low levels of academic quality attained in U.S. elementary and secondary schools. These reports dealt with a most serious problem; hence education again was to become a national issue, attracting the irate attention of the media. The wrath of political leaders followed with an intensity that had not been seen since the Soviets launched Sputnik in 1957.

During this same period, IBM Vice President and Chief Scientist, Dr. Lewis Branscombe, and his colleagues on the National Science Board, the policy-making body for the federally funded National Science Foundation (NSF), were engaged in discussions designed to produce programs to strengthen precollege science and mathematics instruction. Branscombe then served both as Chair of the National Science Board and as head of the Special Commission on Precollege Science and Mathematics Instruction.

In late 1982 the Commission issued a report indicating that science education in the United States was grossly inferior to that in many other countries, most notably in the Soviet Union (National Science Board, 1983). The report recommended a series of programs for the NSF to initiate to remedy this condition at both the elementary and secondary school levels. The NSF programs were to include research and demonstration science education projects. These recommendations were welcomed by the Reagan Administration and Congress, and they were quickly implemented.

By the summer of 1983, the NSF was funding proposals in its now greatly expanded science education programs. Branscombe's leadership in establishing these programs was widely acknowledged. The results, therefore, of the various investigations of education and the promptings and activities of the NSF created a reinvigorated environment in secondary education that welcomed innovations, and particularly those involving the application of technology.

The second general factor pertinent to the establishment of the IBM Secondary School Computer Education Program was the widespread success of the new microcomputer industry. Since the late 1970s, remarkable growth had been shown in developing this product line, and Apple, Radio Shack, and many others had been quick to enter the market. When IBM introduced its PC in August 1981, there was much speculation whether it could ever catch and equal the forerunners in this exciting competition.

The IBM PC, however, received rave reviews in the technical and commercial press. Also IBM's reputation for quality made its PC the most sought after computer for office applications and placed it favorably to compete for both home and school markets. Many software developers hastily converted their packages to take advantage of the IBM PC's memory capacity and 16-bit central processor.

The success of IBM and other vendors of microcomputers in large-scale production and sales resulted in rapid decreases in retail prices. This brought the price of computing down to a range that for the first time most schools could afford.

During late 1982 and early 1983, a trend toward increased private/public collaborations to improve education emerged. This constituted the third general factor previously mentioned. The most visible example of this trend was a bill relevant to computer education introduced in the U.S. House of Representatives by California Democrat Peter Stark. At the urging of Steven Jobs, who at that time was Apple's Chief Executive Officer, the Apple Computer Corporation became interested in donating one microcomputer to every elementary and secondary school in the United States. Congressman Stark proposed federal legislation to provide a substantial tax incentive for any computer manufacturer who might make such donations. When Stark first introduced his bill in late 1982, there was a significant groundswell of support. However, over the next several months, substantial opposition to the bill emerged, and it was never reported out of the House Education Subcommittee. Opposition centered on the wisdom of providing tax relief to one of the nation's strongest industries, particularly at a time when public concern was mounting over the growing federal deficit. Furthermore, many educators expressed concern over the utility of providing incentives for the donation of hardware, recognizing that hardware alone was not sufficient to promote effective school use of microcomputers. A comparable bill introduced in the Senate suffered a similar defeat.

When it was certain that the Stark bill would not pass, Apple pursued the matter in the California legislature and was successful in getting state corporate tax reductions for donations to California schools. Jobs initiated the "Kids Can't Wait" program and began distributing an Apple IIe to any California school that requested one. Apple's actions marked the beginning of large scale private/public collaborations to improve education. Several other vendors soon followed suit.

By early 1983, IBM was actively engaged in discussions with representatives of several outside agencies, including ETS, seeking their advice on the type of computer education program IBM might initiate. ETS staff encouraged IBM to design a comprehensive program that could build upon and expand the earlier private/public partnerships.

PROGRAM DESIGN

At ETS, we were interested in a program to ameliorate some of the conditions identified by the authors of the various critical reports and by the National Science Board. We anticipated that a substantial portion of any IBM donation would provide PCs for schools. We were also convinced that a major part of the resources should be expended for both software and training. IBM wanted the program to be fully operational by the time schools opened for the 1983–1984 school year. ETS staff were concerned that it would be extremely difficult, if not impossible, to design and implement a quality program in such a short time.

Several of the early discussions focused on which grade levels should be included in the program. We considered including the elementary and middle school grades. However, at that time, there simply was not sufficient software available for the PC to be used effectively in these grades. For this reason we limited the program to the secondary level.

Because schools in the United States have organized themselves into so many different combinations of grade levels, we decided to define *secondary school* as any organization that enrolled primarily adolescent students and conferred certificates or state-approved high school diplomas to students who met specified minimum requirements. This definition meant that almost all public, independent, and church-related high schools would be eligible to participate.

In subsequent discussions we agreed that the program should be a pilot effort to identify and exemplify practices encouraging effective educational use of computers. Furthermore, the program would not be one that attempted to evaluate the effectiveness of computer-based instruction compared to traditional teaching methods. At this point in the discussions IBM revealed that it had decided the program should be funded at a level of $8 million. This was surely a momentous decision: A private corporation was funding a multimillion dollar project to benefit public and private high schools.

IBM also indicated that the pilot project would be located in three states—California, Florida, and New York. These states were chosen because together they account for almost 20% of the nation's secondary school pupils. Furthermore, IBM had substantial operations in each state—New York is the home of IBM corporate headquarters and several other major installations, Boca Raton in Florida is the manufacturing site of the PC, and San Jose in California houses a major IBM facility.

IBM and ETS then decided on another feature of the program that was to have a major influence on its design: We had to establish where in each of the three states the participating high schools would be located. We were concerned that schools receiving PCs might experience technical problems beyond their capacity to resolve. At that time no one had much experience using PCs in high schools. Although these machines had tested out as extremely reliable in the laboratory as well as in offices, colleges and universities, and homes, no one knew how they would stand up to the intense use and possible abuse that might occur in high schools. Therefore, we wanted to be certain that all schools receiving PCs were located near a major IBM facility so that systems engineers could conveniently come to the aid of schools experiencing technical problems. Thus, this decision dictated the geographical location from which participating schools would be selected. In California it was the San Jose and Los Angeles areas; in Florida the Boca Raton and Tampa areas; and in New York the New York City, Poughkeepsie, Yorktown, and Binghamton areas.

Subsequent discussions between IBM and ETS in early 1983 produced three other important factors of the program—networks, layered teacher-training, and use of the PC as a tool to facilitate learning. We strongly felt that all high schools in the program should be organized into small groups, or networks, of an average size of seven, to share the knowledge and experience gained from mutual participation. Each network was furthermore to be coordinated by a teacher-training institute (TTI) whose responsibility would be to train the high school teachers for 1 month in the summer of 1983 and to provide network support services during the entire 1983–1984 school year. TTIs in each region then would be selected on the basis of their relative experience and expertise in teaching secondary school faculty to use microcomputers.

Each school was to send from three to five teachers and administrators to the summer training at the TTI. This requirement was established to ensure that the computer education programs would be stable despite the staff turnover that inevitably plagues U.S. secondary schools, particularly among personnel proficient in teaching computing.

In addition to the summer training, the TTIs were also to convene regular meetings of the high school staff in their networks to share knowledge and experiences, provide additional training on new software and applications, and to serve as a general resource and technical backup for the schools. ETS and IBM were also prepared to serve as additional resources for dealing with both educational and technical problems. If the support relationships were to develop effectively, it was apparent that the schools and the TTIs needed to be near each other. The decision was thus taken to specify that all participating schools should be located within 1 hour's travel distance from the TTI coordinating the network.

The second major component in the program design that emerged from the discussions between IBM and ETS in early 1983 was "layered training," a simple concept entailing three levels of training. The first level was the training that ETS staff gave to two representatives from each of the 12 TTIs. The second level was the training provided by the TTIs to the three to five faculty members from the 89 participating high schools. The third level was the training offered by the high school faculty to their own pupils.

The first-level training took place during a 2-week period in May 1983 in Princeton, New Jersey. The second-level training took place during the summer months of 1983 at the various TTIs. Third-level training occurred, of course, throughout the 1983-1984 school year. However, an important part of the program design was ensuring that training would be ongoing.

The final guideline for program design upon which IBM and ETS agreed was the pedagogical assumption underlying the way PCs would be used in the high schools. It was clear that the paucity of software appropriate for use with the PC even at the secondary level in early 1983 was a major concern in program design, for it would be a disservice to give schools hardware and software that teachers could not readily use. Such a prospect brought back unpleasant memories of disastrous programs in the 1950s and 1960s purporting to promote the use of audiovisual equipment and teaching machines.

Research completed by ETS staff and others (Campbell & Gulardo, 1984; Lockheed & Frakt, 1984; Miura & Hess, 1983) showed that most computer education in U.S. secondary schools consisted primarily of teaching white, middle-class males to write programs in the BASIC language. IBM and ETS agreed, therefore, that their major goal would be to promote widespread use of the PCs by a mix of pupils, adding particularly, minorities and females. Thus, training at all three levels emphasized adopting the PCs in as many different academic areas as possible. The primary concept was to use the computers as tools to promote learning in all high school subjects. For example, ETS and TTI staff would encourage the use of word processing in English classes, database management in science and social studies classes, electronic spreadsheets in business education classes, and graphics in art and vocational education classes. The teaching of programming languages such as BASIC, FORTRAN, LOGO, or PASCAL would not be discouraged, but the IBM project would emphasize using generic application software packages rather than developing programming skills.

We also intended to encourage using the machines and software in a variety of extracurricular activities. For example, we hoped that the machines would be used in the production of school newspapers, literary journals, and similar projects. Furthermore, we promoted the use of computers in maintaining statistical records of school athletic team performance or for financial accounting of student activities and agencies. In summation, we were interested in promoting the greatest possible use of the donated equipment by the largest number of students.

1. BACKGROUND AND DESIGN OF THE PROGRAM

PROGRAM GOALS

To reiterate, the purpose of the IBM program was to design and refine a model of effective microcomputer use in secondary schools. To accomplish this purpose, we formulated the following specific goals:

1. Select a group of schools with diverse characteristics;
2. Increase student access to microcomputer hardware and software within these schools;
3. Increase the use of computers across a variety of subject areas, especially those in which computers have not been traditionally used;
4. Increase the number of teachers trained to use computers in education; and
5. Increase the number of support relationships between secondary schools and local teacher-training and other educational institutions.

The remainder of this book describes the extent to which these specific goals have been attained in the IBM program.

2 Selection of Program Participants

Hugh F. Cline

This chapter documents the procedures employed in selecting all the institutions that participated in the IBM Secondary School Computer Education Program. As described in the first chapter, the program design specified the clustering of high schools into networks, averaging seven schools each. At the center of each cluster, a teacher-training institute (TTI) would provide both instruction in techniques of effective educational use of computers and various support services for the high school faculty, administrators, and students in that network. Hence, the task of selecting program participants involved choosing both TTIs and secondary schools.

In the next section of this chapter, we discuss the procedures used for selecting the 12 TTIs that participated in the program, and we identify each TTI and its location. In the third section, we discuss the rather complex process of choosing high schools for the program from among all those that might have been invited. Finally, we give a profile of the schools included in each network and provide summary statistics of the major characteristics of the participating schools.

TTI SELECTION

As mentioned previously, an important aspect of the original program design called for all TTIs and high schools to be near a major IBM facility. In early 1983, when the program was designed, we had very little experience using the PC in secondary schools. Consequently, we were concerned that hardware and software problems might arise that the participating schools, and perhaps the TTIs as well, would not have the resources to resolve. Therefore, we wanted all program participants to be situated near a major IBM facility, where there would be an ample supply of systems engineers to aid in solving technical problems.

In Florida two sites were chosen, each in the southern part of the state. Each was to have two networks. The greater Miami area was selected because of its proximity to Boca Raton, the manufacturing site of the IBM PC; similarly, the greater Tampa area was chosen because IBM has a major data center operating there.

In New York State four sites were designated. The first site was New York City, for it was difficult to conceive of a program in this state that would not include its major city and the opportunity it offered to work within a large, heterogeneous urban school system. IBM also has many facilities in the five boroughs of New York City, including the new IBM Building in midtown Manhattan. The second site chosen was relatively affluent, suburban Westchester County, lying north and east of New York City. Here are located IBM's corporate headquarters, in Armonk, and a major IBM research facility, in Yorktown Heights. The third site was Poughkeepsie, on the Hudson River, about 50 miles north of New York City and the home of one of IBM's largest manufacturing plants. This site provided an opportunity to include urban, suburban, and rural schools. The fourth New York site was Binghamton, in the center of the state and renowned as the place where Thomas Watson Sr., the founder of IBM, had built his first plant. Like Poughkeepsie, Binghamton provided a mix of urban and rural schools.

In California, as in Florida, two locations were designated. The first was the greater Los Angeles area, where IBM has several regional sales and service units. Here, too, the prospect of establishing a challenging model program in a large urban system was most attractive. The second California location was the greater San Jose area just south of San Francisco. Frequently called "Silicon Valley" because of its numerous high technology companies, it is the home of IBM's major West Coast research facility. In both the Los Angeles and San Jose areas, it would be possible to include a diverse group of high schools.

The design of the model program was completed by March 1983. The IBM and ETS program directors then visited the three chief state school officers to brief them on the design and intention of the program and to seek their approval and support. Because these chief state school officers are among the pioneers of technology in education, their wholehearted support was readily obtained.

These visits also initiated effective working relationships between the program staff and those in each state department of education who were concerned primarily with promoting effective use of educational technology. Many of these individuals subsequently provided extensive assistance in selecting TTIs and secondary schools, for they were well informed about the strengths and weaknesses of the programs in institutions throughout their respective states. Furthermore, it was most helpful to learn their plans for promoting effective computer use, for we then were able to avoid conflicts and to ensure instead that our efforts were complementary.

From the earliest stages of designing the computer education program, we recognized that the institutions selected as TTIs would need considerable prior experience and expertise in training secondary school teachers in effective educational use of microcomputers. The exceedingly tight time schedule of the program allowed only a very short period for training. Hence, it was obvious that we needed to select institutions that already had experienced staff.

In summary, two major criteria were used in selecting TTIs for the program. The first was prior experience and faculty expertise in the computer training of secondary school teachers. The second was proximity to the designated IBM installations. Proximity was defined as within 1 hour's travel distance.

The first step in TTI selection, then, was to identify all institutions that met our criterion of *proximity*. We used a number of different sources in creating lists of potential TTIs, including state departments of education and local IBM community-relations personnel.

An additional and largely unanticipated source for names of potential TTIs resulted from the attention paid to the program by the mass media. Following the visits to the chief state school officers, IBM released an announcement of the program to the media. The news that IBM was donating to schools hardware, software, training, and support worth $8 million proved to be of great interest, and the announcement was picked up by the wire services. Many local newspapers throughout Florida, New York, and California ran the story and thus gave the program high visibility. Consequently, IBM and ETS were bombarded with telephone calls, letters, telegrams, and even personal visits from individuals volunteering their organizations.

Using these sources of information, we drew up lists of all possible TTIs in each of the 12 locations. We then applied our second criterion, *prior experience and current expertise* in training high school teachers in computer education. We obtained information on prior experience and current competence from the state education departments and from reviews of college catalogs and course descriptions. As might be expected, we came up with more than one candidate TTI in many locations. At that point we began to look for heterogeneity on selected characteristics among the potential TTIs. For example, we wanted to get a mix of public versus private, large versus small, urban versus rural, and preservice versus inservice institutions. The diversity we sought among the TTIs in the program on the last dimension meant that we wanted to include some institutions that provided only preservice training, some that provided both preservice and inservice training, and some that provided only inservice training.

In Florida, where counties and school districts are one and the same, district offices are the primary agencies for inservice training. In New York, nonprofit organizations, which operate independently of local school boards, offer on a cost-reimbursement basis several services to school districts, including continuing or inservice training. These organizations are known as Boards of Cooperative Educational Services (BOCES), and there are at present 43 distributed throughout the state. In 1983 the New York State Commissioner of Education, Gordon M. Ambach, designated six BOCES as special units for training teachers in computer use and to generally promote more widespread and effective use of microcomputers in schools.

In California, at the urging of then Governor Edmund G. Brown Jr., 15 Teacher Education and Computer Centers (TECCs) had been established in 1982 and given the specific mandate to increase and improve school use of computers. Therefore, in addition to considering all colleges and universities with undergraduate and graduate teacher training programs, we also considered the county offices in Florida, the BOCES in New York, and the TECCs in California that were within 1 hour's travel distance to our 12 designated sites.

The results of our TTI selection process are shown in Table 2.1.

On the east coast of Florida, we chose Florida Atlantic University, which is north of Miami in Boca Raton, and Barry University, in the southeastern sec-

TABLE 2.1
Teacher-Training Institutes

Florida

Polk County School District, Bartow
University of South Florida, Tampa
Florida Atlantic University, Boca Raton
Barry University, Miami Shores

New York

Queens College, Flushing
Putnam/Northern Westchester BOCES, Yorktown Heights
Vassar College, Poughkeepsie
Broome-Tioga BOCES, Binghamton

California

Los Angeles Teacher Education and Computer Center, Downey
Pepperdine University, Malibu
Santa Clara Teacher Education and Computer Center, San Jose
San Jose State University, San Jose

tion of Miami. Both of these institutions had highly regarded teacher training programs in computer education. On the west coast, we chose the University of South Florida in Tampa, also widely known for the quality and extent of its computer education program. The second TTI in the Tampa area was the Polk County School District, situated in a rural area inland from Tampa on the Gulf Coast.

This is the only TTI in the program that is a school district. We wanted to have one network comprising mostly rural schools, and the area east of Tampa was most attractive for this purpose. Because there were no adjacent teacher-training colleges, universities, or intermediate units, we decided to employ the district office as the TTI.

In New York City, we selected a unit within the City University of New York, the Office of Microcomputer Use, in the School of Education at Queens College. This Office had just been designated as one of the Computer Education Technical Assistance Centers by the New York State Department of Education. In Westchester County, we selected the Putnam/Northern Westchester BOCES, an intermediate unit that had already established a reputation for the quality of its computer education programs.

In Poughkeepsie, we selected Vassar College as the TTI. Vassar does not have a program that grants degrees in education, but it is one of several private colleges that recently established programs allowing liberal arts majors to enroll in studies leading to teacher certification. The designers of the Vassar program had decided earlier that it should specialize in computer education. By the time the IBM program was being launched, Vassar had already accumulated credibility in this field. The fourth TTI selected in New York was the Broome-Tioga BOCES in Binghamton. Like Queens College, this BOCES had also been selected by the state department of education to serve as a Computer Education Technical Assistance Center.

In California, two TTIs were selected in the San Jose area. One was the Department of Instructional Technology in the School of Education at San Jose State University. This department had recently established a graduate program in computer education and was drawing to it many teachers in the locality. The other TTI selected was the Santa Clara TEC Center, one of the units established by the state department of education to implement computer education programs.

In Southern California, the two TTIs selected were the Los Angeles TEC Center in Downey, the eastern section of Los Angeles, and the Graduate School of Education and Psychology at Pepperdine University in the affluent West Los Angeles area. The Los Angeles TEC Center was also established as one of the 15 state centers for computer education. The Pepperdine University unit, situated in a private university, already had several years' experience in running a master's degree program targeted to provide teachers with instruction in effective computer use.

Reviewing the entries in Table 2.1, we can readily see that the TTIs were heterogeneous. Seven of the 12 TTIs are institutions of higher education. Of these, four are public, and three are private. Four TTIs are intermediate units, and one, Polk County in Florida, is a school district. This TTI and one other, Broome-Tioga BOCES in New York, are in the most rural of the TTI settings. The other TTIs are rather evenly distributed among large and small urban and suburban localities. The issue of the demographic characteristics of the program participants is discussed in much greater detail at the end of this chapter, where we summarize the background characteristics of the secondary schools.

By the end of March 1983, the 12 TTIs had been identified, invited, and enrolled in the program. As a condition for their participation, the TTIs agreed to serve as the coordinating agency for computer education training and support activities for the secondary schools assigned to their networks. To prepare for this role, the TTIs would send two faculty members to attend an ETS institute for teacher trainers later in the spring. The TTIs would also conduct a month-long training program for three to five teachers and administrators from each of the participating secondary schools and their networks. Last, the TTIs agreed to conduct monthly network meetings for the secondary school staff and generally to support computer education activities in their schools.

In return for these services, the TTIs received from IBM a donation of hardware and software that was similar to that received by the secondary schools. Recognizing that the TTIs would incur substantial costs in meeting their obligations to the program, IBM also donated $10,000 to each TTI to offset partially these expenses. All TTIs were encouraged to use the hardware and software they received to generate additional revenues by offering courses and training programs to any interested individuals. In this fashion, use of the donation might be extended to larger audiences.

This discussion completes our review of the process of selecting the TTIs for participation in the program. We turn now to a similar review of the more complex process of selecting the secondary schools.

SECONDARY SCHOOL SELECTION

The major concern that guided the selection process for secondary schools was proportional representation (i.e., a concern that the schools included should be broadly representative of all secondary schools in the United States). Therefore, the program was intended to have the same proportion of inner city, parochial, or affluent schools as the nation at large. By choosing schools to achieve proportional representation, we would have some basis for generalizing about the utility of our approach. The dimensions chosen to achieve this representative distribution were these:

1. Location — urban, suburban, or rural.
2. Auspices — public, private, or church affiliated.
3. Socioeconomic status of the community served.
4. Racial and ethnic composition.
5. Size of the student body.

For each school, we needed data on the five characteristics just noted. Unfortunately, neither complete listings of schools nor the relevant descriptive data existed. However, Market Data Research (MDR), a market survey firm in Westport, Connecticut, had for several years collected relevant data from all U.S. public schools having a twelfth grade. Their data included variables that could be used as indicators or proxy measures for four of the five characteristics needed for representative selection.

The MDR database included information on location, auspices, and size. Although it did not have data on the level of affluence of the communities served, MDR did include a variable that estimated the proportion of students in each school who came from families with incomes below the federally defined poverty level. We decided to use this measure as a surrogate for community socioeconomic status. However, a more serious problem with the MDR data was the absence of any information on the racial and ethnic composition of the student body. Furthermore, we could not find other databases that included such information. Given the time and resources available to launch the program, we had no other choice than to use the MDR database and solicit help from the TTIs, the local IBM community representatives, and, in some cases, the staff in the state departments of education to inform us of the racial and ethnic composition of schools in their respective areas.

Having opted to use the MDR database, we purchased copies of the tapes from the firm's latest survey, Spring 1982, for the states of Florida, New York, and California. The next task was to identify all schools within 1 hour's travel distance from the respective TTIs. Schools were listed on the MDR tapes in alphabetical order by county. Using a combination of local maps and assistance from the TTIs, we created an operational definition of the boundaries of the areas that included the schools eligible for selection. In some areas like New York City and Los Angeles, there were several hundred eligible schools; in some of the rural sites, there were as few as eight eligible schools.

Lists of all eligible schools were created for each network and circulated to the respective TTIs and local IBM representatives. These lists included information on location, auspices, poverty level, and size of the public schools. We did not have these data on the church-affiliated or independent schools. The TTIs and local IBM representatives were asked to review the lists and suggest schools for the program. All the IBM representatives made such suggestions. However, the BOCES in New York and the TECCs in California declined the invitations to nominate schools, because they provide services to schools in their respective areas. For them to recommend one school in favor of another would place them in an untenable position. Therefore, with the exception of the two BOCES and the two TECCs, all TTIs submitted their suggestions, in many cases coordinating these with the IBM representatives.

In New York City, special arrangements were necessary for presenting a description of the program to the Board of Education, because it was occupied in selecting a new Chancellor to replace Frank J. Macchiarola, who had stepped down after many years of excellent service. The Board was selecting a new Chancellor in the midst of an intense campaign waged by supporters of several minority candidates. However, the senior staff of the Board were most enthusiastic about participating in the program. Despite the Board members being occupied with matters of succession, the staff succeeded in obtaining their approval and in making recommendations to ETS for participant schools. ETS staff also attempted to obtain input from the teachers' union in New York City.

Selection of schools in Los Angeles was also complicated; in this case, however, the complication was not succession but a financial crisis. In the spring of 1983, the Superintendent and the Board of the Los Angeles Unified School District (LAUSD) were confronted with a projected deficit of several million dollars for the next school year. Thus, it was necessary to consider closing several schools in the system and to bring about some consolidation of existing school catchment areas. Such decisions are always difficult to make, and the advocates of maintaining the existence of some schools over others usually state their positions forcefully and attempt to gather support for their positions. Because of the gravity of its financial crisis, the LAUSD was unable to turn its attention immediately to the IBM program. In fact, it was not until early June that the LAUSD formally agreed to participate in the program and sent us their recommendations for participating schools.

Negotiations for the program in the Los Angeles area were further complicated by some communication problems between the local IBM representative, ETS, and the LAUSD. These problems were caused primarily by our desire to select schools as quickly as possible to ensure sufficient time to choose and prepare teachers for summer training. As had occurred in New York City, the excellent staff of the LAUSD greatly facilitated the review and the participation of their district in the program.

Special negotiations were also required in the Miami area. Because the areas defined by 1 hour's travel distance from Florida Atlantic University and Barry University overlapped in Broward County, it was necessary to coordinate the recommendations received from both the TTIs and the local IBM representatives. Furthermore, discussions were held between the staffs of all county offices in the Miami area to come to a mutually satisfactory allocation of program participation among the relevant districts. The staff in the Florida State Department of Education actively participated in these negotiations.

2. SELECTION OF PROGRAM PARTICIPANTS 17

Supplied with the suggestions from the relevant TTIs, local IBM representatives, and where appropriate, boards and state departments of education, ETS staff then proceeded to select the final program participants. The selection decisions, as noted previously were guided primarily by the need for proportional representation. But in many cases the need for this representation could be satisfied by several schools in an area. In these instances, we were guided by the recommendations received from the many sources already discussed. After ETS made the selections, the names of the schools were recirculated to the TTIs and IBM representatives, and final adjustments were made.

The final selection of the participating schools was influenced by one further consideration: our desire to include among the program participants several schools that served special student populations. We were especially interested in including schools that served the handicapped, native Americans, and students whose educational progress was comparatively slow. Therefore, we asked the TTIs, the IBM representatives, and the state departments of education to suggest names of special schools. The selections ultimately included several such schools in each state, and these are described following.

The original design of the project called for creating four networks in each of the three states. Each network was to consist of seven schools. Thus we planned for 28 schools per state, or 84 schools in the program. In fact, we ended with 89 schools in the program: 29 in Florida, 29 in California, and 31 in New York. The size of the networks ranged from five to nine. These departures from the design were accommodations to local conditions and the different capacities of the TTIs. Table 2.2 lists all the schools in the 12 networks, which we now describe.

On the east coast of Florida, in the greater Miami area, were two networks: one was coordinated by Barry University with nine schools, and one was coordinated by Florida Atlantic University with eight schools. The Barry network was in the southern part of Broward County. This network consisted of nine schools: four public urban and suburban schools, two Roman Catholic schools, a Hebrew school, a private school, and the Miccosukee School for Seminole Indians in the Everglades National Park. This school, administered by the Bureau of Indian Affairs, teaches Seminole Indians, who are enrolled in grades K through 12.

The Florida Atlantic University network covered the northern portion of Broward County and the relatively affluent Boca Raton County. Of the eight schools in this network, five were public suburban schools, two were independent, and one was affiliated with the Roman Catholic Church.

One network on the west coast of Florida was coordinated by the University of South Florida. The seven schools were all public high schools in the Tampa, St. Petersburg, Sarasota, Clearwater, and Plant City areas. All were either in urban or suburban settings, and two had special programs for learning-disabled students, who would be making heavy use of the donated

TABLE 2.2
Secondary School Networks

Florida

Barry University Network
  American Senior High School
  Archbishop Curley/Notre Dame High School
  Boyd H. Anderson High School
  Coral Gables Senior High School
  Greater Miami Hebrew Academy
  Miami Edison Senior High School
  The Pine Crest School
  St. Thomas Aquinas High School
  Miccosukee Indian School

Florida Atlantic University Network
  Atlantic High School
  Boca Raton Academy
  Boca Raton High School
  Deerfield Beach High School
  Lake Worth High School
  Pope John Paul II High School
  The Potomac School
  J. P. Taravella High School

University of South Florida Network
  Boca Ciega High School
  Chamberlain High School
  Countryside Senior High School
  Hudson Senior High School
  Plant City High School
  Plant High School
  Sarasota Senior High School

Polk County Network
  Fort Meade Junior-Senior High School
  Kathleen Senior High School
  Lake Gibson Senior High School
  Mulberry Junior-Senior High School
  Winter Haven Senior High School

New York

Queens College Network
  Brooklyn Technical High School
  John Dewey High School
  Lexington School for the Deaf
  The Manhattan Center for Science and Mathematics
  Martin Luther King Senior High School
  Newtown High School
  Theodore Roosevelt High School
  The Ramaz School
  Susan E. Wagner High School

TABLE 2.2 *(continued)*

Putnam/Northern Westchester BOCES Network
  Brewster High School
  John Jay Senior High School
  The Hackley School
  John F. Kennedy High School
  Peekskill High School
  Yorktown High School
  White Plains High School

Vassar College Network
  Arlington Senior High School
  Beacon High School
  John Jay High School
  Kingston High School
  Our Lady of Lourdes High School
  Poughkeepsie High School
  Roy C. Ketcham High School
  Spackenkill High School

Broome-Tioga BOCES Network
  Newark Valley Junior-Senior High School
  Oneonta High School
  Owego Free Academy
  Seton Catholic Central High School
  Tioga High School
  Union Endicott High School
  Vestal High School

California

Los Angeles TECC Network
  Banning High School
  Bell Gardens High School
  Bishop Montgomery High School
  Diamond Bar High School
  Downey High School
  Garfield High School
  Manual Arts High School
  Valley High School

Pepperdine University Network
  The Brentwood School
  The Downtown Business Magnet High School
  El Camino Real High School
  Los Angeles Lutheran High School
  San Fernando Valley Christian High School
  Santa Monica High School
  Venice Senior High School

(continued)

19

TABLE 2.2 *(continued)*

Santa Clara TECC Network
  Blackford High School
  Half Moon Bay High School
  Los Altos High School
  Menlo Atherton High School
  Monterey High School
  Santa Clara High School
  Soquel High School

San Jose State University Network
  Bellarmine College Preparatory
  California School for the Deaf
  Gilroy High School
  Institute of Computer Technology
  William C. Overfelt High School
  Pioneer High School
  Santa Theresa High School

machines. Our rural network contained only five schools. Because the staff of the Polk County School District, which had no prior experience in computer education, served as the TTI for this network, we made the network smaller to decrease the level of their training and support activities. The five schools in this network were selected from the total of eight rural public high schools in Polk County.

In the state of New York, network size varied from seven to nine schools. The New York City network, directed by Queens College, consisted of nine schools: five large urban public high schools — one in each of the five boroughs that make up New York City — a public technical high school, a high school for deaf students, a newly created magnet school in Harlem whose program focused on science and mathematics, and a private Hebrew academy. The Putnam/Northern Westchester BOCES included seven schools: six suburban high schools and an independent school whose students aspire to enroll in highly selective colleges and universities and have the benefit of an already established excellent program of computer education. The Vassar College network consisted of eight schools: seven public urban and suburban high schools and one secondary school affiliated with the Roman Catholic Church. The Broome-Tioga BOCES network comprised five public suburban schools, one small independent school, and a Roman Catholic school.

In California, 29 schools were included in the program. As in Broward County in the Miami area, schools in the LAUSD were divided between two networks, the Los Angeles TECC and Pepperdine University. The TECC network included eight schools. Seven were inner city or suburban public high schools, and one was affiliated with the Roman Catholic Church. Among the public schools in the TECC network was one special institution, known in California as a continuation school. California state law requires every district to provide facilities to instruct all students through age 18. Most districts comply with the law by maintaining a continuation school. These schools are usually small and offer special programs. Typically, two kinds of student attend continuation schools. The first are those students who have experienced minor behavioral or disciplinary problems usually associated with poor attendance records. The second are very gifted pupils who, because they frequently find regular school programs boring, are not performing well.

The Pepperdine network contained seven schools. Three were public schools in relatively affluent urban and suburban areas. Two of the schools were affiliated with Protestant church groups, and one was an independent school serving students from primarily middle-class and upper-middle-class families. The last school in the Pepperdine network was an LAUSD magnet school in the downtown business section of the city. Students came to the magnet school from all over the district, some being bussed for 2 hours each way. The magnet school's program emphasized business education, but it also offered a complete college-preparatory option.

In the San Jose area were two networks, one administered by the Santa Clara TECC and the other by San Jose State University. The TECC network included seven public high schools distributed within the city of San Jose, the suburban towns, and the rural areas to the north and west of the city. The San Jose State University network also included seven schools. Four were public urban and suburban high schools, one was affiliated with the Roman Catholic Church, and the remaining two were special schools—a public school for deaf students and a school offering a unique program in computer technology.

As soon as the school selection procedures were completed in each network, letters of invitation to participate in the program were issued by IBM. The letters were hand delivered by the local IBM community-relations staff. In most instances, the letters were given to the school principal or headmaster. Where two or more schools from the same district were included in the program, the invitations were delivered to the superintendent. The first invitations were issued in Florida in late March, and the last were delivered in Los Angeles in early June. All the schools that were invited to participate in the program responded positively.

Commitment to participate in the program was confirmed in a letter of agreement between IBM and the schools. The letter was very brief and primarily asked that the schools agree to maintain the operating status and security of the computers.

In many instances, the acceptances were preceded by extensive deliberations on the part of the schools and occasionally protracted negotiations between TTIs, IBM, and ETS, because the schools were asked to agree to provide specific contributions to the program from their own resources. This policy of matching or partial matching of grant monies is commonly employed by many public and private funding agencies. The rationale for such policies is that grantees will value more highly the received funds if they also invest something of their own in the shared effort.

This policy was also implemented in the IBM Program. However, rather than require that each school contribute a fixed sum of money to the program, we thought it more appropriate to require the school to comply with guidelines designed to ensure that the program attained its goals. On these matters we wanted an informal agreement with the schools. Therefore, the requirements were communicated to the TTIs and schools in memoranda from ETS and were not elevated to a legal status by inclusion in a contract letter.

The guidelines included the following:

1. Send three to five teachers to a 4-week training program at the TTI during the summer of 1983.
2. Compensate teachers for their participation in the summer training according to existing local policy.
3. Send the principal to a 2-day training session during the summer of 1983.
4. Establish a building-level computer education coordinator (compensation or release time for this position strongly recommended).
5. Design and provide an inservice training program for other faculty.
6. Develop or revise a statement of goals and objectives for the school's computer education program.
7. Develop or revise the short-range and long-range plans for achieving the computer education goals and objectives.
8. Establish adequate budget allocations to provide ongoing support and growth for the program.
9. Provide adequate site preparation and space allocation to house the computers and software.
10. Provide adequate security for hardware and software.
11. Send teachers and administrators as appropriate to the regularly scheduled network meetings.
12. Solicit, coordinate, and submit student and faculty contributions to the program newsletter.
13. Submit interim and year-end reports as requested.

In any program with as many organizational participants as the IBM Computer Education Program, there is bound to be substantial variation in both the degree of compliance with program guidelines and success in attaining program goals. The extent of these variations and the factors we consider important in having caused them are described in later chapters. However, before concluding this chapter describing the procedures employed in selecting program participants, we briefly report summary statistics of the secondary schools.

STATISTICAL SUMMARY

Table 2.3 presents data comparing the distributions of the 89 high schools in the IBM program with the distributions of all public high schools in the United States on the variables of size, location, auspices, and poverty level.

TABLE 2.3
Profiles of Participating Schools

School Variables	IBM Program (All Schools)	IBM Program (Public Schools Only)	U.S. Total
Size of Student Body			
2,500 +	16%	20%	3%[a]
1,000 to 2,499	48%	56%	30%
500 to 999	25%	20%	26%
−500	11%	4%	41%
Locations of Schools			
Urban	32%	27%	18%[a]
Suburban	47%	47%	27%
Rural	21%	26%	55%
Auspices of Schools			
Public	79%		76%[b]
Church-related	8%		17%
Independent	13%		7%
Proportion of Students from Families Below Poverty Level			
25% +		10%	21%[a]
12% to 24%		46%	34%
5% to 11%		27%	32%
−5%		17%	13%

[a]Data on size, location and poverty level for the U.S. total are abstracted from the 1982 Market Data Research Survey and include only public schools with a 12th grade.

[b]Data on auspices for the U.S. total are abstracted from the 1980 survey conducted by the National Center for Education Statistics, reported in U.S. Department of Education, *Digest of Education Statistics* (1982).

The only database from which we could draw relevant information on these variables was the one collected by MDR. Because MDR surveyed only public schools, our comparisons are flawed. Therefore, we have added to Table 2.3 the middle column, which reports distributions of the 70 public high schools included in the program.

Looking first at distribution of the schools on the basis of the size of the student enrollment, the reader sees that we have overrepresented large schools and underrepresented small schools. Among the nation's public high schools, only 3% enroll more than 2,500 students. But in the schools included in this program, 20% of the public and 16% of all the schools enroll more than 2,500 students. Correspondingly, 41% of the public schools in the nation enroll fewer than 500 students; and of the total 89 schools in the program, only 11% are so small. Clearly, the schools included in the program have larger enrollments than those of the high schools in the nation at large. This overrepresentation of larger schools was recognized and encouraged during the selection process. The recommendations received from TTIs, local IBM representatives, and state departments of education all favored larger schools.

This overrepresentation of larger schools permitted more students to participate in the program. This decision resulted in overrepresentation of urban and suburban schools at the expense of rural schools, for it is primarily the rural schools in the United States that have small student enrollments. As shown in the table, 55% of U.S. schools are in rural areas. In the IBM program only 21% of the schools were in rural areas. Of the public schools in the program, only 26% were rural. It is possible that the operational definitions of *rural* used by the two agencies that collected these data were not the same. But the differences are so large that we can safely conclude that our program overrepresented urban and suburban schools at the expense of rural schools. Given the correlation between size and location of schools, this finding is not at all surprising. However, as mentioned previously, the preference for larger and urban schools was recognized and fostered, because the result was the involvement of more students.

For school affiliation, the match of distributions is very close between the nation's high schools as reported by the National Center for Education Statistics (NCES) and the participants in this program. As indicated in Table 2.3, there is an overrepresentation of independent schools: 13% in the program compared to 7% nationwide. This imbalance is also reflected in the underrepresentation of church-affiliated schools in the program: 8%, compared to 17% in the nation. These differences in auspices are relatively small; thus, we conclude that we at least attained diversified, if not strictly proportional, representation on the dimension of school affiliation.

The final characteristic for which we sought proportional representation was *level of affluence* of the community served by the school. Data on this dimension proved to be the most difficult to obtain. For the church-affiliated and independent schools, the concept of the community served was different from that of the public schools. For public schools, only the MDR data could be used as a substitute indicator of affluence.

As shown in Table 2.3, the match in distributions between public schools in the nation at large and those public schools included in the program is reasonably close. If any imbalance exists at all, we have slightly underrepresented those schools in which large proportions of students are from families whose incomes are lower than the federally defined poverty level. Because the poverty level of a community is directly related to the resources available to support schools through local taxes, it is likely that the TTIs, the local IBM representatives, and the state departments of education showed some preference in their recommendations for schools with more resources available to support the program. Consequently, they expressed a slight bias against higher poverty-level communities. However, the differences are sufficiently small to permit our concluding that our program is broadly representative of the schools in the nation at large with respect to the level of affluence of the communities served.

SUMMARY

In this chapter we have identified the criteria, described the procedures, and enumerated the TTIs and secondary schools selected for participation in the IBM program. We have also examined descriptive statistics characterizing the schools. We concluded that the schools in the program overrepresent the larger and consequently more urban and suburban schools in the nation. However, they are a reasonably accurate representation of the nation's schools with respect to auspices and level of affluence of the communities served. It is also clear that we achieved our goal in obtaining a highly diverse collection of secondary schools to participate in the program, thereby giving us the opportunity to observe the operation of the program in widely varying settings.

In the following chapter attention is turned to configurations of hardware and software donated to the TTIs and the high schools.

3 Hardware and Software Selection

Roger C. Kershaw

In a program of this magnitude, the hardware and software selected are crucial to success. Much thought was therefore given to developing a configuration of hardware and software appropriate for secondary schools. This chapter discusses the hardware and software items selected for the program, the reasons for the choices, and such related issues as security and maintenance. The participation of third-party hardware and software vendors is also described and discussed.

In selecting the hardware and software components of the donation, ETS was strongly influenced by several discrete aims: (a) promoting equitable access and use by minority groups and women; (b) eliciting a sense of ownership in the program on the part of the schools; (c) facilitating continued use of the hardware and software in the schools beyond the 1983–84 school year; and (d) ensuring that school curricula would not be directed, or perceived as being directed, by ETS. In the following sections, further explanations are given of how these aims affected selection of both hardware and software.

HARDWARE SELECTION

The hardware configuration chosen for the schools had to meet two practical criteria beyond those listed previously. First, the equipment had to be available in sufficient supply from existing IBM inventory to meet the very tight delivery schedule imposed by this program. IBM announced the program in March of 1983, thus leaving only 6 months in which to carry out all ordering, shipping, and installation activities for the 12 TTIs and 89 high schools. Second, the number of computers to be donated to each school had to be compatible with the overall plan. The program plan specified that all donated PCs be kept together in the high schools in centralized laboratories. Each school would receive a sufficient number of PCs for the labs, promoting easy and equitable access by classes of students.

Most computer education programs have been the exclusive province of advanced mathematics and science students. With the IBM program, teachers in every discipline would, by design, have the opportunity to bring their classes to the lab and use software relevant to their subject areas. By ensuring that all subject-area teachers would have access to the hardware and appropriate software, the program would promote more widespread and equitable use of microcomputer technology within the schools.

The program design provided for a laboratory of 15 IBM PCs to be donated to each high school. We arrived at the number 15 because the average class size in U.S. schools during the 1982–1983 school year was approximately 28.5 students. We considered it reasonable for two students to use a computer in a laboratory setting. In fact, we strongly suspected that two students per machine would stimulate greater student interaction. We believed that greater student interaction would result in richer learning experiences and increase the speed with which pupils would become proficient in using the software "tools."

Initially, we proposed that adjustments be made in the actual number of machines to be donated to each school, depending on specific school characteristics and typical class sizes. In the final implementation, however, this allowance for class size was used only at the Miccosukee Indian School in Dade County, Florida. Here, the total high school student population was fewer than 60 students; consequently, their donation amounted to four IBM PCs and one printer.

ETS convened a panel of educational technology experts in the spring of 1983 to review and comment on the design of the training, network support, and hardware/software package. At this meeting, described in more detail in chapter 4, one of the main conclusions reached was consensus on the typical configuration of computers, peripheral equipment, and software for each high school.

Hardware Components

For each high school in the program, IBM shipped the following collection of hardware items:

1. Fifteen IBM PCs each with 2 single-sided diskette drives, and 128,000 bytes of read/write memory.

3. HARDWARE AND SOFTWARE SELECTION

2. Fifteen keyboards.
3. Fifteen IBM Color Monitors and appropriate system unit adaptors.
4. Three IBM Graphics Printers, including the appropriate IBM PC printer port mounted in the system unit, printer cable, and printer stand.

Later in the evolution of the project, data communications capabilities were added to the aforementioned equipment. The included components were a communications board, a modem and cable, communications software, and access to a national information utility for each institution. Most important, the data communications facility would allow the schools to participate in an electronic mail network in which schools could share database files, lesson plans, and information on student experiences. After several solicitations were made by ETS to various vendors, and after IBM approval, the Source Telecomputing Corporation, Tymnet, Inc., and Hayes Microcomputer Products Inc. joined IBM in donating the products and services needed for telecommunications. It was an important addition for vendors like The Source and Hayes to contribute so substantially because, by virtue of their willingness to participate, the vendors reinforced the importance of this effort to the schools.

The configuration for each of the teacher-training institutions was essentially the same as for the high school donation, with only a few exceptions. Five, rather than three, printers were provided to the TTIs. The Hayes Smartmodems contributed to the TTIs were a faster version than were those donated to the high schools. The additional printers and the faster modem were given the TTIs, because we knew they would have greater demands on their facilities in the training programs. The TTIs also received a $10,000 grant from IBM to offset further the expenses incurred by participating in the program. Although these funds could be used to cover any related operational costs, many of the TTIs used the money for additional hardware and software they needed to purchase during the 1983–1984 school year in support of the high school networks.

The donation by Hayes Microcomputer Products Inc., consisted of more than 100 Smartmodems and Smartcom II communications software packages. In addition, Koala Technologies Corporation sent each participating institution the KoalaPad TouchTablet and the KoalaWare software, *the MicroIllustrator*. Using this easy-to-learn system, students can create music, paintings, and drawings with the touch of a finger to the digitizing tablet. Each institution was required to buy a game adaptor board to interface the tablet to their PC and also a copy of PC DOS 2.0 or 2.1. This hardware/software combination gave the schools another dimension in computing for use with their IBM PCs: graphing with a digitizing tablet.

The participation of additional third-party software vendors in this donation program is discussed further in the next section.

Hardware Maintenance and Security

In the beginning of this chapter we emphasized our interest in promoting equitable access, in building a sense of program ownership in the schools and in ensuring the continuation of the program beyond the 1983-1984 school year. However, we also did not want to dictate curricular decisions to the schools. As mentioned in chapter 2, we circulated to the schools a number of guidelines for effective computer use, but we did not elevate these issues to the legal status of contractual items. Nevertheless, with respect to certain points concerning the maintenance and security of the hardware, IBM and the schools entered into a letter of agreement for program participation. Before accepting the invitation to participate in the program, each high school official agreed to provide for the maintenance of the hardware and for appropriate preparation of a computer laboratory for each school.

In signing the letter of agreement, each school agreed to: (a) use the PCs for instructional purposes only; (b) certify that the PCs would not be sold, traded, pledged, or otherwise encumbered; (c) provide a suitable laboratory for the computers; (d) be responsible for obtaining and paying for consumable supplies (for example, paper, ribbons, diskettes, etc.); (e) obtain and pay for maintenance of the donated PCs upon the expiration of the normal warranty period; and (f) ensure that the licensed software would not be copied or reproduced in any way.

IBM, on the other hand agreed to: (a) provide the schools with 15 Personal Computers free of charge and pay for their delivery and installation; and (b) license, free of charge, the accompanying software materials.

From the onset of the project, we realized that maintenance and security would be major concerns. The potential for equipment failure with a substantial collection of complex devices in use by high school students was high. Robbery and vandalism posed threats as well.

The IBM PC has proven to be a very reliable machine when used in a business setting; however, its reliability with student users had been largely untested. IBM and ETS agreed early that whatever the schools could do to ensure the uninterrupted use of all 15 machines in the school labs would need to receive high priority if we were to realize our goal of having schools become self-sufficient by June 1984. Eliciting a sense of commitment and ownership from the schools was very important to us, but this objective had to be accomplished through reasonable fiscal demands. Having the schools provide for the lab setup, maintenance, and proper security was one way in which they could demonstrate the desired commitment. Suggestions and typical pricing alternatives for providing maintenance on the PCs were offered to the schools and TTIs. Warranty service was extended by the IBM Service Centers free for the first 90 days following delivery of the PCs. In addition, suggestions were offered to the high schools concerning security. This advice included: (a) having the equipment gathered in one room on the second floor; (b) securing all windows and doors against unauthorized entry; (c) restricting all off-hour access through building coordinators; and (d) using other security precautions such as bolt-down systems, burglar alarms, or additional security personnel.

ETS and IBM provided as much information to the institutions as possible to ensure a successful program. ETS disseminated information to the schools on physical lab requirements, on how to care for the equipment and supplies, and on even more pressing matters like estimates of the budget line items a typical school might be expected to incur (for example, expenses for computer paper, printer ribbons, diskettes, cleaners, a private telephone line, site preparation costs). During the high school training sessions at the TTIs, a short seminar was held on hardware maintenance and service. In addition, a list of maintenance guidelines and information on lab configurations developed by a teacher-trainer from Vassar College was distributed to all of the schools (see Appendix A).

SOFTWARE SELECTION

Background

To meet the program goals and objectives, IBM and ETS provided software that met the following criteria:

1. *Friendliness* in educational settings.
2. Availability from IBM.
3. Availability of supplementary materials to support the software.
4. Compatibility with equipment donated to the schools.
5. Applicability to secondary school subject areas.
6. Availability at the time of the scheduled software shipments.

Although the program was designed to promote widespread use of the computers in many different subject areas by many students, we wanted to give the schools opportunities to make their own informed choices concerning software packages, because these selections would have implications for innovations in the curriculum. Therefore, we decided upon a procedure whereby each school would get a common initial set of software packages and two subsequent opportunities to select additional software. The software for the program was scheduled to be distributed to the TTIs and the high schools at three intervals: a core package of software to be delivered with the equipment followed by two supplements. The supplements were distributed later in the school year after teachers had become familiar with the equipment and could estimate their future needs. The TTIs were included as recipients of the software so that they could support their networks with training programs and software evaluations throughout the school year.

The "core" software packages included were considered necessary to perform the basic functions of the donation project and had value relative to the training and curriculum integration. The categories of software considered for the donation were those software groups typically considered part of generic software for microcomputers, that is, database managers, word processing, spreadsheets, graphics, and programming tools. These licensed program materials along with some reference and tutorial books are listed in Table 3.1.

Table 3.1 enumerates the various tutorials and computer programming packages included in the initial shipment. These packages were provided to ensure that the teachers could get a quick start in using the equipment. The *pfs:File* and *pfs:Report* software were selected in the database management category because this series is extremely easy to use and yet offers im-

TABLE 3.1
Core Software and Reference Material Donations

Software	Number of copies	Description
DOS 1.1	15	the PC operating system
BASIC Primer	15	tutorial on BASIC programming
Typing Tutor	15	typing instruction
Easywriter	15	word processing
pfs: File	3	data base management
pfs: Report	3	report generator
The Instructor	15	Intro to the PC
Question	15	CAI
Computer Discovery	15	computer literacy game
Free Enterprise	1	business game
Arithmetic Games	1	learning game
Books		
Technical Reference Manual	1	PC component specifications
Hardware Maintenance and Service Manual	1	diagnostics

pressive database functions. For word processing, the only IBM-distributed product available at the time was *Easywriter Version 1.1* offered by Information Unlimited Software Inc. Because keyboarding skills for teachers and students were to be rapidly developed in the schools, *Typing Tutor* was added to the list of "core" software. The spreadsheet software was not distributed with the initial shipments because two competitive packages, *Visicalc* and *Multiplan,* were simultaneously available. Because we wished the schools to have the option of making an informed selection, the spreadsheet software choice was deferred until the next "menu" was offered. The *Technical Reference Manual* and the *Hardware Maintenance and Service Manual* were also included so that schools having the technical resources to provide their own repairs could do so without incurring additional expense.

Early in the project, IBM introduced the concept of a software catalogue from which participating schools could select and order software packages. Each high school and TTI had an account with credits that they could use to acquire software from the catalogue. In August 1983, schools received the first of two software catalogues. The second cycle of ordering followed midway in the project after more experience had been gained by the schools. The options contained in the first catalogue or second software delivery are shown in Table 3.2. The participating TTIs and schools chose from this list to complement the core software that they received in September 1983.

In February 1984, participants received the second catalogue shopping list that included the packages shown in Table 3.3. Many packages offered in the core list were also included in the first option list and the final list. The repetition was intentional, for it allowed the participants the flexibility to select as many packages as they needed and to do so when it made the most sense to acquire software based on their curriculum and teacher-training program.

The large number of programming software products on the optional lists were cause for concern among the high school and TTI staff. It is important to understand that the optional software list was generated from the available IBM PC licensed software at the time of the software announcement. There was no conscious decision to favor programming tools over applications software; the list simply reflected the IBM software line then current.

As in the case of the third-party hardware donations, ETS and IBM had invited vendors of computer software products to participate in the IBM donation. It was clear that in order to offer a complete array of software to the schools, we would have to go out into the market to identify programs in graphics, data communications, programming, and other categories beyond those licensed by IBM.

ETS staff had extensive experience in educational software review and selection over the last few years and had established a rapport with many authors and distributors in the educational software market. Through direct solicitation of these vendors, ETS staff were able to arrange for vendors to

TABLE 3.2
Software Option List No. 1

Software	*Description*
Visicalc	Electronic worksheet program
Multiplan	Electronic worksheet
PeachText	Word processing program
pfs: File	Electronic filing program
pfs: Report	Report generation program
Home Budget	Personal accounting software
Professional Editor	Text processor for programmers
Diskette Librarian	Utility program for organizing files
Personal Editor	Text processor
Macro Assembler	8086/88 Assembly Language compiler
ACS Communications Support	Data communications program
IBM BASIC Compiler	for DOS 1.1
IBM Pascal Compiler	for DOS 1.1
IBM Cobol Compiler	for DOS 1.1
IBM Fortran Compiler	for DOS 1.1
UCSD p-system Pascal	UCSD operating system w/Pascal
UCSD p-system Fortran	UCSD operating system w/Fortran
UCSD Pascal Compiler	Pascal compiler
UCSD Fortran Compiler	Fortran compiler
Computer Discovery	CAI computer literacy
Private Tutor	CAI authoring disk
Learning to Program in BASIC	Tutorial on BASIC programming
Arithmetic Games 2	Educational game
Free Enterprise	Educational game for business
Snooper Troops 1	Adventure game — mystery
Snooper Troops 2	Adventure game — mystery
Cross Clues	Reasoning game

TABLE 3.3
Software Option List No. 2

Software	Description
Monster Math	Math game
Adventures in Math	Math game
Snooper Troops 1	(in Optional List 1, also)
Snooper Troops 2	(in Optional List 1, also)
States n' Caps	Geography game
Wordwhiz	Vocabulary game
Wordskills-level 3	Vocabulary game
Wordskills-level 4	
Wordskills-level 5	
Wordskills-level 6	
Free Enterprise	(in Optional List 1, also)
Cross Clues	(in Optional List 1, also)
Computer Discovery	(in Optional List 1, also)
Private Tutor	(in Optional List 1, also)
Learning BASIC	(in Optional List 1, also)
Learning DOS 2.0	Tutorial on 2.0 operating system
Professional Editor	(in Optional List 1, also)
Diskette Librarian	(in Optional List 1, also)
Personal Editor	(in Optional List 1, also)
File Command	Diskette utilities
DOS 2.1	Updated PC DOS operating system
IBM Macro Assembler	(in Optional List 1, also)
IBM BASIC Compiler	(in Optional List 1, also)
IBM Pascal Compiler	(in Optional List 1, also)
IBM Fortran Compiler	(in Optional List 1, also)
UCSD p-system Pascal	(in Optional List 1, also)
UCSD p-system Fortran	(in Optional List 1, also)
UCSD Pascal Compiler	(in Optional List 1, also)
UCSD Fortran Compiler	(in Optional List 1, also)
Logo: Version 1	IBM Logo

(continued)

KERSHAW

TABLE 3.3 *(continued)*

Software	Description
Logo: program	with Turtle Graphics
CBASIC Compiler	Business BASIC Interpreter
PL/1 Compiler	PL/1 Language Compiler
Visicalc 1.2	Updated elecronic spreadsheet
Multiplan 1.1	Updated electronic spreadsheet
Peachtext	(in Optional List 1, also)
pfs: File	(in Optional List 1, also)
pfs: Report	(in Optional List 1, also)
dBase II	Data base management
BPI General Accounting	Business accounting
Home Budget	(in Optional List 1, also)

provide software at no cost or at substantially discounted prices. IBM project staff provided valuable suggestions of software and often facilitated donations by negotiating with the vendors for shipment of software to schools. The following list includes the organizations that contributed to the program and the products they offered.

- Alpha Software Corp. — offered discount on all of their software products to schools
- Computer Access Corporation — donated a graphing program called *Delta Drawing,* published by Spinnaker Software, to all schools.
- Cybertronics International Corp. — donated Karel the Robot, a Pascal teaching tool to all of the TTIs.
- Hayes Computer Products Corp. — contributed, in addition to the modems, Smartcom II communications software to all participants.
- Koala Technology Corp. — contributed the KoalaPad TouchTablet and graphics software to all schools.
- McGraw-Hill Book Company — provided a variety of computer software and book products to the TTIs.
- Science Research Assoc. (SRA) — contributed *Arithmetic Games, Computer Discovery* and *Free Enterprise software.* These packages are also listed in the core package donated by IBM because SRA is an IBM subsidiary.
- Software Publishing Corp. — discounted their entire line of software products, including *pfs:File, pfs:Report, pfs:Graph* and *pfs:Write* to

all of the schools. Copies of *pfs:Graph* were also donated to the 12 TTIs.
- The Source Telecomputing Corp. — gave free accounts and blocks of free access time to all participating institutions.
- Tymnet and the Source worked together to allow schools to access the network without common carrier charges.
- Visicorp, Microsoft, Lotus, and Micropro gave discounts to all qualifying educational institutions on their line of software products. ETS notified the 101 IBM Project schools of their availability and conditions for ordering.

Originally, the IBM donation program was not intended to include third-party gifts and discounts. As the program evolved, however, it became clear that other leaders in the microcomputer industry were very interested in joining with us in providing software and hardware tools for secondary-school use. Each of the vendors listed in Table 3.4 and in the previous section, *Hardware Selection,* market highly visible and respected products that extend the basic goals of the program as we have defined them in chapter 1. The support and enthusiasm exemplified by the vendor donations gave credence to the model of using the computer as a tool in the secondary-school environment.

SUMMARY

This chapter has attempted to capture the hardware and software selection experiences that IBM, ETS, and the participating TTIs and high schools shared in the IBM Secondary School Computer Education Program. Some of the goals that directed the selection of hardware and software were: (a) promoting equitable access and use by minority groups and women; (b) eliciting a sense of ownership in the program on the part of the schools; (c) facilitating continued use of the hardware and software in the schools when the formal donation support ceased at the end of the 1983–1984 school year; and (d) ensuring that school curricula not be a perceived or actual IBM-dictated or ETS-dictated outcome of this program. To achieve these goals, we designed the donation components and lab environment to maximize teacher options in pursuing their own instructional objectives through the use of computers. Providing adequate numbers of personal computers and software packages relative to typical class sizes encourages teachers to bring entire classes to the lab in a regularly scheduled manner. Packages were chosen for their ease of use, so that skills acquisition specific to the software would be minimized. Finally, the range of software packages included a diversity of tools prompting teachers of different subject areas to find packages applicable to their curriculum needs.

Familiarizing the participants with the IBM PC and all the donated software represented a significant training objective for ETS, for the teacher trainers, and for the teachers at the 89 high schools. The complexity of the hardware, the operating system, and all of the applications software signalled a major change to the typical model of computer education in the schools. The next chapter discusses the ETS training model and our experiences relative to the challenges that were faced.

4 Staff Training

Martin B. Schneiderman
Brian Stecher

Microcomputers are coming into school systems at an accelerating rate as educators try to respond to the changing needs of the information age. Yet there is strong evidence that this influx of equipment is outpacing educators' abilities to put micros to effective use. Too often, educators spend their total instructional computing budgets just to purchase the new hardware. In contrast, schools that implement exemplary computer education programs recognize that substantial institutional resources must be dedicated as well to planning, curriculum development, software acquisition, staff training, and continuing support services. Having recognized these factors as essential to success, the IBM Secondary School Computer Education Program made staff training a major emphasis.

IBM announced the computer education program on March 21, 1983, planning for the 1,500 personal computers to be delivered to the 89 schools in time for the opening of school in September. ETS staff were thus faced with the challenge of quickly designing and conducting a faculty development program. Clearly, to have the greatest impact on the largest number of educators in a brief period of time, it was necessary to design a program with a multiplier effect; that is, ETS would start with creating and training a small group of teacher-trainers, who would in turn train another small group, and so on.

ETS, therefore, began with developing 24 teacher-trainers, two from each of the 12 participating teacher-training institutions, a cadre that went through an intensive 2-week course in May 1983. During the next 3 months, the TTIs conducted 12 four-week-long summer institutes that were attended in all by 482 high school teachers, school principals, and district administrators. This chapter describes the training institutes and identifies the common characteristics of programs that we considered to be the most successful.

TRAINING THE TEACHER-TRAINERS

Selecting the Participants

Once the 12 teacher-training institutions agreed to participate in the program, they were invited to send two faculty members to attend an intensive 2-week teacher-trainer institute, conducted at ETS. The program took place during the last 2 weeks in May 1983 so that participants could also attend the Fourth Annual National Educational Computing Conference in Baltimore the following week.

ETS recommended that the choice of staff members from each institution be based on the individual's ability to conduct the regional summer institute for secondary school teachers and to provide comprehensive network support to the participating secondary schools during the 1983–1984 school year. For these reasons, it was recommended that attendees have experience in teacher training, using and teaching about microcomputers, and secondary level curriculum and instruction.

The Teacher-Trainers

The 24 individuals who attended the ETS institute represented a wide range of backgrounds and experience. Job titles included the following: college professor, assistant superintendent, math teacher, science teacher, county computer education coordinator, computer consultant, and computer literacy project coordinator. Although many participants were already using computers and teaching their use, their formal training and academic degrees represented many different disciplines including anatomy, biology, chemistry, computer education, computer programming, earth science, education, educational administration, educational psychology, elementary and secondary curriculum development, English, futuristics, geography, holography, instructional communications, mathematics, metallurgy, natural science, paleontology, physics, physiology, political science, psychology, science education, sociology, and statistics.

None of the trainers had substantial experience with the IBM PC, although many were quite familiar with Apple, Atari, Radio Shack, Commodore and other microcomputer systems. In spite of our request for experienced microcomputer users, 7 of the 24 participants had little or no experience in using or programming *any* microcomputer.

The Institute Program

The purpose of the institute was to prepare each team of trainers to develop and conduct the summer teacher-training program for the secondary school teachers in their network. In addition, the participants would be taught how to establish and support their local network of secondary schools. Trainers would also be responsible for follow-up training sessions throughout the year and for assisting the secondary school teachers to develop and conduct inservice programs for other faculty members in their schools.

The goals and objectives for this institute were developed during the winter of 1983 and refined in April with the assistance of five project advisors, chosen for their experience in training computer educators. The advisory group included: Gary Bitter, Arizona State University, Tempe, Arizona; Bobbie Goodson, Computer Using Educators, San Jose, California; Arthur Luehrmann, Computer Literacy, Inc., Berkeley, California; James Poirot, North Texas State University, Denton, Texas; and Susan Talley, Total Information Educational Systems, St. Paul, Minnesota.

The general goal of the institute was to show teachers how using the IBM Personal Computer and applications software could enhance traditional courses and extracurricular activities. The specific goals and objectives set for each team of TTI trainers are presented in Table 4.1.

The Instructors

Primary instructors for the institute were Randy Bennett, Director of the ETS Technology Lab; Roger Kershaw, Director of the ETS Technology Research Group; and Martin Schneiderman, Director of ETS Computer Education Programs. Together, this team drew on their experience in elementary and secondary classroom teaching, special education, curriculum development, school administration, teacher training, program evaluation, educational research, computer programming, telecommunications, system design, and hardware maintenance. Other ETS staff members as well as consultants and industry representatives made presentations during the 2-week program.

Instructional Format

A unique aspect of this teacher-trainer institute was that it focused on the computer as a general-purpose tool; it did not teach programming nor promote computer-assisted instruction. Instead, the participants explored applications of microcomputers in a variety of secondary school disciplines and extracurricular activities.

TABLE 4.1
May 1983 Teacher-Trainer Institute Goals and Objectives

Curriculum Integration

Discover uses of word processing, database management, graphics, and spreadsheet programs in different subject areas.

Learn to integrate the use of microcomputers into secondary school programs.

Teacher Training

Create a plan for teaching the use of applications programs in various subject areas.

Develop a comprehensive schedule for a teacher-training program.

Develop materials and techniques for teaching teachers about the IBM PC and its uses in secondary schools.

Network Support

Develop plans for establishing and maintaining a school support network.

Develop plans for obtaining and maintaining the support of secondary school principals for the program.

Software

Become familiar with the operation of a wide range of applications software packages, tutorials and learning games including:

EasyWriter 1.1	Computer Discovery
Word Proof	Visicalc
PFS: Graph	Multiplan
The Instructor	Question
BASIC Primer	Smartcom II
PFS: File	Snooper Troops
PFS: Report	Arithmetic Games
	Free Enterprise

Examine a broad range of instructional courseware, applications software, print, and audio-visual materials for the PC available from third-party distributors.

Develop plans and techniques for helping teachers select and evaluate appropriate computer-based instructional materials.

Telecomputing

Access commercially available on-line databases.

Use an electronic mail network.

Computer Languages

Become familiar with the three versions of IBM PC BASIC and how they differ (i.e., Cassette, Disk, and Advanced BASIC).

Become aware of those commands and structures that differentiate IBM Advanced BASIC from other popular dialects of BASIC.

Know about the existence of other programming and authoring languages for the PC (e.g. Cobol, Fortran, and Pascal).

TABLE 4.1 *(continued)*

Hardware Operation

Develop a working knowledge of the components that make up the IBM PC.

Learn how to set up the IBM PC and run system diagnostics.

Diagnose common hardware and software problems.

Learn how the PC is different from other micros currently available in schools.

Perform routine preventive maintenance to system components.

Operating System

Perform common housekeeping operations using PC-DOS 1.1 (e.g., formatting, checking, and copying disks; comparing files and disks; erasing and renaming files; transfering DOS and BASIC to software).

Recognize the difference between external and internal PC-DOS 1.1 commands.

Create batch and automatic execution batch files with PC-DOS 1.1.

Develop an understanding of IBM PC system utilities and their purposes.

Peripheral Devices

Become familiar with peripheral devices useful for educational purposes (e.g., graphics tablets, card reader, plotters, speech synthesizers, light pens, etc.).

Become familiar with interfacing common peripherals to the PC.

Every attempt was made to provide a working environment in which teacher-educators would encounter few obstacles and enjoy being learners. The schedule for the 2-week institute was extremely ambitious. On the first day participants were provided with their personal computers in the original shipping boxes. The first task was to work in teams to inventory software, unpack hardware components, assemble systems, and run diagnostic programs. As many remarked, the day seemed like "Christmas in May."

Formal presentations by ETS instructors were designed to demonstrate how a user could be "up and running" with a software package as quickly as possible. Sample data, text, graph, and spreadsheet files were distributed during the demonstrations and used for practical exercises and open lab time. ETS staff also paid particular attention to detail and gave each participant a comprehensive set of materials including training manuals, reprints of articles, reference books, directories, bibliographies, blank diskettes, and highlighter pens to annotate documentation.

At the conclusion of each session the group was reconvened to brainstorm different ways that students and teachers could use the application software packages. The group also discussed innovative teaching and learning strategies.

The instructors joined participants for almost every meal and were available during the open lab sessions after dinner. The participants worked at their computers late each evening and on the weekend, developing secondary school applications of the software and exploring the capabilities and limitations of the hardware.

The Training Site

The institute was held at the Henry Chauncey Conference Center on the ETS Princeton campus, 400 acres of wooded countryside, an hour's drive from New York and Philadelphia. Undoubtedly, the setting for the institute was critical to the success of the program.

ETS selected the site so that participants would be living and working together for the full 2 weeks, free of job and family responsibilities. Each learner-teacher was provided with his or her own microcomputer and 24-hour access to the computer lab, a library of applications software, instructional software, curriculum materials, audiovisual materials, and peripheral devices.

The program was conducted in a large conference room containing 17 IBM Personal Computer stations around the perimeter of the room and a demonstration system at the front. Near this large room were two smaller rooms, one containing an additional eight computer systems arranged in two "islands" of four stations. The third room served as a library, demonstration area, and conference room.

Two microcomputer systems were used for large-group and small-group presentations. Both system configurations included peripheral devices and large-screen, high-resolution monitors. The systems are described in Table 4.2.

Hardware and Software

Each participant received at the outset seven boxes containing the components of the computer system, software, and course materials. As noted, the first task was to inventory the contents of the boxes and then to work in teams to unpack and assemble the hardware. On the last day of training, the cartons were repacked and shipped to each participant's office or residence.

Participants' Evaluations of the Training

At the conclusion of the institute, participants were asked to evaluate the training program. The instructors were judged to be "knowledgeable, well prepared, organized, good-natured, and responsive." Many participants commented favorably on the attention given to the planning activities, others approved of the flexibility shown during all aspects of the training and saw it as important to the success of the program. The "tone" of the training was de-

TABLE 4.2
Hardware Configurations Used for
Group Instruction

IBM Personal Computer (2)

128K memory
dual disk drives
high resolution RGB color monitor
parallel printer card
asynchronous communications card

Peripherals

IBM Graphics printer
Qume letter quality printer
IDS Prism color printer
Votrax Speech Synthesizer
HP 7470a plotter
Symtec light pen
Hayes Smartmodem

Large screen monitors

Barco 26" RGB Color Monitors (2)
Ball 25" high resolution monochrome monitor

scribed as "focused, informative, and well-balanced" in both content and format.

The rapid tempo, on the other hand, was a major source of frustration, although most participants acknowledged the need for intensiveness. Several participants mentioned that the open lab hours during evenings and weekends compensated for the rapid pace of the formal presentations.

The group structure, which permitted and encouraged a prolonged sense of community for generating ideas and drawing on each others' strengths, was much appreciated. Several trainers noted that the diversity of their backgrounds and experience made interactions more effective. There was a sense of regret that the interactions would be difficult to continue and maintain once the teams left Princeton.

The presentations by outside speakers drew criticism. Only some were perceived as informative or engaging. A few participants cautioned against allocating much premium time to outsiders.

The issue of outside speakers raised the more generalized question of how the available 2 weeks could have been better planned. Suggestions included offering more assimilation time, more "hands-on time," and fewer, or more limited, formal presentations. Although the participants agreed that the demonstrated software had been extensive and appropriate, they suggested more dialogue on secondary school curriculum issues, e.g., development, implementation, and strategies for integrating the microcomputer with educational programs. A few suggested the potential usefulness of presession handouts and outlines, and ideally, of supportive background materials distributed even before the training began.

All felt that the Henry Chauncey Conference Center facilities at the ETS Princeton campus had helped the training to succeed. As one participant remarked: "Critical thinking develops within a comfortable, relaxed atmosphere . . . the accommodations and service promoted concentration . . . (There was) nothing in the world to worry about except learning."

In summary, the teacher-trainers expressed satisfaction that surpassed all expectations regarding their personal and community goals, their appreciation of "patient instructors, hospitable staff, and an observant IBM contingent," and their gratitude at having been invited to this "landmark event."

TRAINING THE TEACHERS

Summer Institutes for Secondary School Teachers and Principals

A condition of participation in the program was that each TTI must conduct a "comprehensive 4-week training program," which each was free to design and schedule. As a result, there was considerable diversity in the schedules and daily routines at the 12 sites.

Staff from the Polk County Teacher Center were the first to begin their program, starting on June 13th; most of the other TTIs commenced their institutes in early or mid-July. ETS strongly encouraged the TTIs to begin their programs no later than mid-July so that teachers would have the rest of the summer at home with their PCs to work at developing materials that could be used during the school year.

While six of the institutes ran for four consecutive weeks, five of the TTIs opted to schedule two 2-week sessions, with a block of time between in which teachers took their computers home to work on projects. The Westchester/Putnam BOCES ran its program during the first 3 weeks in July and reconvened the group for the last week in August. Barry University elected to divide the teachers into two smaller groups and conducted two 3-week programs, each with one trainer.

When ETS visited the training sites during the summer, teachers expressed a clear preference for training institutes that began early in the summer, thus providing them with ample time later to have the PCs at home for independent use. One teacher said, "Having the PC at home contributed immeasurably, and to me was the most exciting aspect of the course."

On the other hand, TTI trainers felt that a later start offered them more time to plan and prepare the training program. Ideally, the ETS institute should have been scheduled earlier in the year; however, given the compressed schedule that governed the entire program, this alternative was not possible.

Staffing

In most cases, the two trainers from each TTI who attended the program in Princeton were the primary instructors at each of the summer institutes. In addition, many of the instructors enlisted the help of guest speakers, who were colleagues, graduate students, or teachers attending the summer program.

For example, the staff at the University of South Florida established a cadre of teacher-instructors, the Teacher Support Group (TSG), who assisted in planning and executing the training. Each TSG member received an IBM PC to take home for 2 weeks before the summer institute so that they could design and write learning packets for each of the software packages. During this process they became familiar with the hardware, operating system, and selected applications software packages. Teachers were divided into teams of "instructional groups" that were chaired by TSG members. During lab time, TSG members were available to answer questions and assist individual group members. As each teacher became proficient in using a software package, he or she was required to "check in" with the TSG teacher before proceeding to another activity. In this way, each participant was allowed to progress at his or her own rate. This arrangement also distributed the responsibility for instruction among a larger number of individuals, thereby freeing the primary TTI trainers for individualized instruction.

Team-teaching arrangements were very effective. Instructors assisted each other during formal presentations and responded to unanticipated matters such as solving technical problems, interfacing peripherals, setting up audiovisual equipment, and arranging for photocopies.

In two of the summer institutes the instructors chose not to team teach; instead, they "departmentalized" instruction. This choice occurred because of differences in teaching style and conflicting teaching commitments. We observed that this approach did not result in as much continuity as the team-teaching model provided and was therefore less effective.

The Institute Participants

Each of the participating high schools was invited to send as many as three to five teachers to the summer training, because secondary schools usually have relatively few "computer using" teachers. Therefore, we were convinced that for IBM's innovative program to be successful, these schools would need to establish a "critical mass" of teachers possessing computing expertise.

In fact, as revealed by a survey that ETS conducted, principals in the participating high schools reported that before the summer institute training, an average of only three teachers per school were "highly qualified" to teach about computing. Principals also reported that fewer than 1% of their teachers had majored or minored in computer science, and only 6% of their entire faculty had taken *any* college-level courses in either instructional computing or programming. Hence, a goal of the program was to increase this number of teachers and also to ensure that teachers in many different subject-area specialties would become proficient at using microcomputers.

The number of educators, who were trained at each site, ranged from 27 to 45; the average was 36. In all, 482 educators attended the 12 summer programs.

ETS strongly encouraged principals and headmasters to select teachers from diverse subject areas. Slightly more than half (51%) of all the training participants represented the four high school subjects that have traditionally been associated with instructional computing (i.e., math, science, business education, and computer science). However, the remaining 49% of the participants were from 28 other subjects. English teachers (10%) and school administrators (7%) were well represented as were women: 47% of the participants were female.

Instructors reported that most of the participants had little or no experience in using microcomputers and that, as a group, math teachers had more background in operating and using computers than their colleagues. Table 4.3 details the teachers' subject-area specialties.

Training Sites and Computer Labs

Each of the 12 TTIs received IBM personal computers, graphics printers, and multiple copies of software while the instructors attended the May institute in Princeton. Also delivered to each site were approximately 21 additional PCs that, at the conclusion of the summer institute, became part of the donation to each high school.

Each TTI was free to decide how these microcomputers would be used during training. Some TTIs chose to set up their labs with all 36 machines, one per teacher. One TTI opted to set up its teaching lab with the 15 PCs that belonged to the TTI; the remaining computer systems were sent home with teachers during the first week. If five teachers came from the same high school, they were asked to take turns using the computers during the summer.

TABLE 4.3
Subject Matter Areas of
The Summer 1983 Institute Participants

Subject Matter Area	Male	Female	Total
Architecture	1	0	1
Biblical Studies	0	1	1
Business	12	42	54
Computer Coordinator	2	0	2
Computer Science	7	7	14
Data Processing	2	0	2
Distributive Education	1	0	1
Economics	1	0	1
English	13	36	49
Foreign Language	5	4	9
Guidance	2	3	5
History	3	2	5
Home Economics	0	3	3
Industrial Arts	6	0	6
Journalism	1	0	1
Language Arts	2	2	4
Law Studies	0	1	1
Library	1	2	3
Life Sciences	1	0	1
Media Specialist	1	1	2
Math	63	49	112
Music	1	1	2
Physical Education	0	2	2
School Administrators	30	2	32
Science	48	18	66
Secretary	1	1	2
Social Studies	14	10	24
Special Education	4	14	28
Vocational Education	2	2	2
	256	226	482

Teaching the Teachers

Many of the summer institutes made adaptations and improvements to the ETS training model. The major mode of presentation at all the TTIs was a hands-on approach rather than reliance on lectures and large-group presentations. Instructors at one TTI indicated, "Applications were introduced via lecture/discussion, with the majority of the teachers' time spent with the manual and machine. This process soon became known as M&M learning."

Many of the summer programs began their day at 9:00 a.m. and concluded by 4:30 p.m. However, at almost every site, teachers chose to arrive early and stay late. The instructors at Florida Atlantic University reported that teachers at their site spent particularly long days in the lab:

> It is interesting to note that we had built frequent coffee and stretch breaks into our instructional plan. The teachers ignored them—they wanted to remain at the microcomputers and work. On several occasions, we (TTI staff) ordered a halt to activities, powered down the machines and requested all to take a break. We needed the break even if the teachers did not.
>
> The scheduled daily period for the summer TTI was originally set to begin at 10:00 a.m. and end at 4:30 p.m. with an hour for lunch. Also the lab was open during the evening hours for special projects, usually closing at 9:00 p.m. However, at the teachers' request, we opened the lab at 8:00 a.m. and changed the lunch period to 30 minutes. The lab continued to be open at night.
>
> From this observed data, we can positively conclude that teachers, given an IBM Personal Computer and appropriate software, do not have to eat, drink, or use restrooms. A heretofore undiscovered characteristic of a teacher.

Queens College in New York City conducted its sessions each day from 7:30 a.m. to 12 noon, thus sparing the teachers the rush-hour traffic. The College's staff paired teachers at the computers so that the remaining 21 PCs could go home with teachers, on a rotating basis, from the first week.

We observed that several TTIs began each day with a brief group meeting at which the previous day's activities were reviewed, announcements made, and questions answered. These sessions helped the teachers to become a more cohesive group and the TTI staff to adjust instruction better to specific needs. The trainers at Pepperdine University described a ritual that became an important part of each morning's "opening exercises":

> One teacher presented a so-called tip of the day on the second day of training. This idea caught on immediately, and that teacher was asked to provide a tip of the day *every* day. Suggestions ranged from discussions of new hardware to listing the 800 (telephone) number of an insurance company that provided home insurance for PCs at reasonable rates.

Two of the TTIs assigned their teachers to keep a daily diary using EasyWriter. Teachers were encouraged to describe what they had accomplished that day and also to express how they felt about learning to use a microcomputer. For many teachers the TTI provided their first experience in using computers. The instructors at the University of South Florida, therefore, found the approach to be extremely effective:

> At the end of each day participants completed a record of daily events. Not only were teachers obtaining greater skills in the use of a word processor but they were also able to record both cognitive and affective reactions to the training.
>
> . . . Under the cloak of anonymity, it was hoped that participants would express concerns or frustrations that they might be unwilling to bring up in group meetings.

By reading the teachers' logs each night, the instructors were able to tailor their presentations and consequently respond effectively to individual and group needs.

Integrating the Applications Software

Teaching teachers to use generic applications software in the different academic disciplines proved to be more difficult than many of the instructors had anticipated. Several of the instructors reported that teachers wanted "real software," i.e., instructional courseware in the discipline they were teaching. In response to this demand, ETS staff developed and distributed to all institutions databases that contained descriptive information on instructional courseware available for the IBM PC. These datafiles were created using PFS:File and PFS:Report, the database management software provided to all schools.

Although most teachers had little difficulty learning to use the applications software, few were able to develop substantial applications of the computer during their initial summer training program. Not all the summer institutes succeeded in helping teachers develop strategies and plans during the 4-week period to integrate the computers with existing courses. One teacher commented that, "It was unfortunate that more concrete examples of how we can use it in the classroom were not generated during our course."

We observed that the programs we considered most successful established special-interest groups (SIGs) of teachers for secondary-level subjects. This grouping allowed teachers to spend time brainstorming and refining their ideas. This "crosspollination" resulted in more and better ways of using the computer in the different disciplines. Many instructors explained that at the end of the month-long program, many of the teachers were just becoming comfortable with the hardware and software. They expected that teachers would begin integrating computer applications with their courses throughout the 1983–1984 school year.

The teachers and administrators reminded us that it would be difficult to revise their curricula and "retrofit" existing courses in the weeks remaining before the opening of school. Many looked forward to offering their students new or modified courses in the following school year.

Projects and Applications

Curriculum-based projects that integrated the applications software were the backbone of the training, for it was through them that cooperative teams were built and materials useful to the entire group were completed. Some projects were undertaken to make it easier to teach students how to use the software; others were designed to complement units in secondary courses. Table 4.4 presents some of the projects and applications that were developed by the teachers during the summer.

The Importance of Social Interaction

Some of the TTI trainers recognized the importance of encouraging social interaction among the teachers early in their month-long training programs. The value of this informal interaction should not be underestimated. Instructors scheduled group luncheons, pot-luck dinners, and family picnics. One site even had a "family day" where any teacher's family or friends were welcome to come to the training to find out at first-hand what the teachers had been accomplishing.

Teachers at Queens College designed and ordered silk screened T-shirts to read "DOS IS GOOD" on the front with "TO THE LAST BYTE" on the back. On the final day of the program at Vassar College, teachers put on skits and sang.

Institutional Support

After staff visited each of the 12 summer institutes, we concluded that the level of institutional support provided by each TTI's host institution differed substantially. It was also evident that the level of institutional support directly affected the program's outcome.

In one case, the instructors did not know whether they would be paid for any of the time that they prepared for and conducted their summer program. At this institution, the department chairman charged a larger order of floppy diskettes to his personal credit card so that the materials would be available when the teachers arrived. An instructor at another institution reported that the cost of supporting the program was much higher than anticipated: "The expenses to the TTI host institution were prohibitive. Much selling of the 'soul' had to be done to encourage the administration to help out. The TTI coordinator was at the mercy of the university administration who did not fully understand the nature of the program."

In other cases, we encountered TTIs that had invented "creative" ways of circumventing unfruitful administrative policies and procedures, in the interests of making the program absolutely first rate. It was evident that the instructors who had the attention, understanding, recognition, and support of the key administrators in their institution were able to direct their energies and time to designing and offering a training program of high quality.

The teacher-trainers from the Polk County network believed they had a distinct advantage (as compared with the other TTIs) because they were employees of the same county school system as the participating high schools. It was much easier to arrange for teachers' stipends, travel expenses, release time, site preparation, and maintenance agreements, because all administrative and budgetary decisions fell under the jurisdiction of a single district administrator and school board.

Administrator Involvement and Commitment

Computer education programs will not succeed without support of a building principal and district administrators. Some of the instructors were successful in involving these key institutional decision-makers in significant ways. However, for many of the TTIs, this area was one that warranted greater emphasis.

Pepperdine University, for example, invited each building principal to spend a day with his or her teachers at the beginning and end of the program. During this time the principals learned how to operate the IBM PC. For many of the principals, it was the first time that they had ever used a computer. Teachers were directed to "keep your hands in your pockets or else sit on them!" This carefully orchestrated day also provided principals with an opportunity to learn about their teachers' plan for using the lab of 15 microcomputers with their students the following September.

The purpose of this important show-and-tell session was to get the principals to "buy into the program," for their support and commitment would be invaluable in the months to come. As teachers and principals began their discussions, it quickly became apparent that substantial amounts of scarce or costly institutional resources would be required to support the program. In particular, the teachers told their principals that the principals would need to:

1. Recognize the capabilities and the limitations of the technology.
2. Provide release time and substitute coverage so that teachers could attend the regularly scheduled network meetings.

TABLE 4.4
Projects Developed by Teachers During the Summer Institutes

EasyWriter and Volkswriter International

Teachers created lesson plans, schedules for in-service programs, site preparation requirements and correspondence.

Teachers kept daily diaries.

Foreign language teachers created document in French and Spanish.

Question

(A computer version of the "21 Questions" learning game)

Teachers created Question datafiles of: famous people, trees, polygons, famous quotations, periodic table of the elements, musical instruments, and units of measure.

PFS:File, PFS:Report and PFS:Graph

A teacher and his son created records and generated reports for a paper route.

Teachers created a database of information about students including: name, address, grade, counselor, class schedule, work experience, school activities, business courses completed, records of absences, tardiness and truancies.

A science teacher created a database of science software for all popular microcomputers.

An instructor created a database containing information about nations of the world including: name, continent, population, area, population density, major manufactured goods, major agricultural products, literacy rate, mortality rate, number of teachers, etc. PFS:Graph was used to read and create graphs to analyze information contained in a database about nations of the world.

Teachers created a database of library books to support the reading program of high school students.

An earth science teacher developed a database of minerals for students to use in identifying specimens in a geology course.

A science teacher created a database of the elements.

Teacher trainers and teachers created databases and graphs of data on the summer institute participants.

An English teacher created bibliographies of books for students to search by title, author, subject or keyword.

A health teacher created a database of drug modifiers.

A social studies teacher conducted a survey and analyzed data concerning political party preferences.

A librarian created a database of IBM PC hardware components and serial numbers.

A computer coordinator created and maintained a database of stock inventory by item number, description, quantity, unit, price and vendor.

A teacher conducted and analyzed survey data concerning characteristics of successful marriages.

4. STAFF TRAINING   55

TABLE 4.4 *(continued)*

A physical education teacher measured and compared cardiovascular fitness as a result of various physical activities.

A history teacher analyzed data from a survey of newspaper articles.

An English teacher analyzed data from a survey of Shakespeare's plays.

A teacher created a database for students to record and graph weekly records of the number and types of errors in English composition.

A genetics teacher created and analyzed data concerning inherited traits.

A physics teacher analyzed and graphed laboratory data from a physics experiment about pendulums.

Visicalc and Multiplan

A teacher created an electronic spreadsheet template to record and report student grades.

A business education teacher created a student activity fund accounting spreadsheet.

Delta Drawing

A teacher used Delta Drawing to design school logos and posters.

A geography teacher created a map of the Western Hemisphere.

A chemistry teacher created a picture of organic molecules and electron dot diagrams.

A teacher created a picture of an airplane with labels of control surfaces.

A science teacher created a picture of ecological food chains and webs.

BASIC Programming

A teacher wrote a BASIC program to play "The Flight of the Bumblebee."

A math teacher wrote BASIC programs to teach concepts in trigonometry.

A teacher wrote BASIC programs to keep a record of students' grades.

---

3. Rewire the computer lab.
4. Install deadbolt locks, Plexiglass on windows, and a security system in the computer lab.
5. Adapt, build, or buy tables for the computer lab.
6. Release teachers from hall, bus, or study-hall duty to staff the computer room.
7. Hire aides to supervise the computer lab.
8. Purchase a maintenance agreement or self-insure against equipment failure—typical cost being 12% of the retail cost of hardware per year.
9. Budget for many consumable materials, including floppy diskettes, paper, and ribbons.
10. Budget for acquisition of new software and peripheral devices.

11. Install a telephone line so that the school can access The Source.
12. Provide release time or stipend for faculty members who are designing and conducting in-service computer education for other faculty members.
13. Provide a stipend for a Computer Education Coordinator.

It is important to note that each school and district that accepted the donation of hardware and software from IBM also agreed, as a condition of participation in the program, to provide substantial support for the program. Despite that, many principals were surprised at the extent of support they were being asked to provide.

Teacher Compensation

We believed that teachers who were paid to attend the summer institute would increase their commitment to the program. Consequently, one of the prerequisites for accepting the donation from IBM was that each school was required to "compensate 3-5 teachers for their participation in the four-week summer training program as per school/district policy."

Some of the TTIs reported that on the first day of the summer institute, teachers compared their various rates of compensation and thus discovered a large difference among them. Some large city public and some private and parochial schools offered no compensation to their teachers, whereas other schools paid their teachers more than $1000 to attend the month-long training program. Some teachers resented this inequity, believing that they should receive equal pay for equal work. ETS and TTI staff explained that the differences were owed to each district's contract or policies and that IBM believed that each school should assume the responsibility for compensating its own staff members. TTIs reported that these concerns became less important as programs got underway.

COMMON CHARACTERISTICS OF THE BEST SUMMER INSTITUTES

Activities

It is difficult to identify all the factors that contributed to the effectiveness of the 12 educational programs, yet there were several programmatic features common to what we perceived as the most successful institutes. Our findings are based on site visits, interviews with teachers and principals, and a case study of the training experience (Stecher, 1984a, 1984b).

The single most important factor was the decision to provide *extensive hands-on practice with the computers.* In many of the institutes, participants spent a minimum of 50 hours operating the computer and becoming familiar with the software. Even so, most teachers considered themselves, at the end of the training, to be only advanced novices. Participants were encouraged not only to work on the machines in the classrooms, but also to take them home during the summer to gain additional practical experience.

The participants also responded enthusiastically to the opportunities for *teacher interaction.* As noted previously, teachers were given special projects to complete in school groups and in SIGs that cut across school lines. This work encouraged collaboration and fostered the formation of communication networks. Opportunities for teacher interaction were the most frequently praised element in the inservice programs.

Another important element in the success of the teacher institutes was their strong emphasis on *planning for implementation.* Some computer education activities focus only on hardware and software. In contrast, these IBM institutes stressed not only development of lesson plans for using the technology in the classroom but also the institutional implementation plans for integrating computers with the educational program at the school.

One reason it was possible to accomplish so much was that the instructors had *clear goals and objectives* for the program. Consequently, the instructors could design specific activities to achieve these goals and were successful in imparting useful skills to teachers.

Careful planning was evident from the detailed *schedule of activities* that participants received at the beginning of their program. This schedule served as an advance organizer, so teachers knew what topics would be addressed, when certain questions were going to be answered, and when free time would be available. It also duplicated the type of planning teachers are typically asked to do for their own classes and thus reinforced the reassuring idea that the instructors were experienced educators.

In our view, the most successful approach to presenting new computer-related skills was *structured lessons.* Typically such lessons began with clear directions, continued with a shared example of the product or process, provided opportunities for individual exploration, and concluded with a related assignment. In contrast, lessons with a minimum of introduction and a greater amount of open discovery left many people confused and frustrated. Remarks from teachers who received less structured lessons confirmed this impression.

One effective instructional strategy was *software-based assignments,* furnishing opportunities for participants to become very familiar with and adept at using particular pieces of software. For example, each participant was required to keep a daily diary using the word processor. There were no rules about what had to be included in the diary, but the assignment had to be completed using the software.

An alternative approach that some trainers selected was to give unstructured time for teachers to practice whatever computer skills they wished. The drawback of this approach was to assume that all participants could act as self-directed learners, set appropriate goals, and create their own activities. When the subject matter is new, and somewhat fear-provoking as it can be in the case of computer technology, these tasks can be very difficult. Hence, the specific software-based assignments may generally constitute the more effective approach for inservice training.

The only serious objection to participation in the training came from teachers who were not voluntary participants and did not expect to be involved in computer-related activities in the next school year. These people were somewhat less enthusiastic than the other teachers, and they did not appear to benefit from the institute as much as the other participants.

The instructors in the most successful programs paid much *attention to the social needs* of the group, and their concern appeared to have a very positive effect. For example, freshly brewed coffee was available every morning at no charge; picnics, open houses, and dinners for participants' families were all arranged. These extra personal touches seemed to increase the espirit de corps among the teachers and also provide a tangible demonstration that the participants were considered respected professionals.

One significant advantage that derived from scheduling the inservice program during the summer was that there were *reduced distractions* from work. Participants devoted more time and attention to the inservice training because they were free from other responsibilities. It was possible to arrive early and stay late, and most elected to do so on a regular basis. The corollary for midyear inservice training is to maximize convenience in scheduling so that one isolates the computer-learning activities from outside pressures and distractions.

Facilities and Equipment

Sufficient computer hardware and software permitted each of the teachers full access to a computer whenever it was necessary. No one was required to share equipment, learn in groups, wait in lines for access, or feel rushed to accommodate others.

The machines in this inservice program were identical to the computers the teachers and students would use when they returned to their schools. Consequently, everything the teachers learned about the hardware was directly applicable to their school situation, and all the software ran exactly as it would in their school. The *similarity of the computers* to the equipment available in the teacher's own school enhanced the effectiveness of the program.

Great care went into the selection of *appropriate software.* The software matched the goals of the program and was not too complex for school use. In this instance, all the participants had access to general application software like word processors, spreadsheets, and database management programs that had been selected for their appropriateness to teacher and student needs.

In the more effective institutes, the *classroom facilities* were large enough and well enough arranged for effective inservice training. One large laboratory generally accommodated all the computers and printers, and had sufficient additional space for storing software. In addition, two or three standard classrooms for lectures and group meetings away from the computers were often used. Overall, the total classroom space used in the effective summer institutes was almost twice what would be required for a noncomputer program.

Two other features of the computer laboratories were noteworthy. First, indirect lighting was preferred. Headaches and eyestrain can be a serious problem when video terminals are used in improperly lighted surroundings. Second, comfortable padded swivel chairs with arm rests were available. Those who sat in front of a computer for 4 or 5 hours a day came to appreciate these chairs; the teachers showed no evidence of the lower back pain that can come from long hours at the computer.

As may be imagined, much *logistical support* was necessary to make these programs successful. In addition to the facilities just discussed, the best programs also benefited from supplemental staff and equipment made available by the host institution. These supplements included help from other faculty members, software librarians, graduate students and technicians, as well as access to large software libraries and other microcomputer facilities.

Personal Characteristics

Just as in any other educational endeavor, the success of a computer inservice program depends on the skills and abilities of the trainers. Of course, fundamental teaching skills are essential—among them the ability to express oneself clearly, to present ideas in a logical sequence, to understand and respond to feedback from students, and so on. Beyond these skills, however, are specific traits and abilities that are related to effective computer inservice training.

Trainers needed, obviously, to have a thorough *knowledge of microcomputers.* Beyond their general knowledge of microcomputer operations, instructors also needed familiarity with the *educational uses of computers.* Knowledge of business or scientific applications is not an effective substitute for familiarity, among other topics, with computer literacy, computer assisted instruction, and computer management of education.

Another important characteristic demonstrated by the project's successful instructors was their *familiarity with teaching*. The instructors had been teachers themselves and were acquainted with the problems encountered by teachers. For example, a module on planning for implementation grew out of the trainer's own knowledge of the process of change in schools. This unit proved to be one of the most important parts of the training project.

A critical boost to the success of the program was the instructors' *respect for the teachers as professionals*. (Apparently such respect is not always evident during inservice education programs.) It is easy to imagine why respect is an important concern in computer education. Technologically sophisticated individuals have an unfortunate reputation for "talking down" to audiences who are unfamiliar with computers. The arrogance of specialists can be a serious obstacle in any information exchange, and particularly in an inservice program.

The best instructors acknowledged the skills and abilities of the trainees and treated them as fellow professionals. A typical comment from one of the instructors captured their attitude: "Let's face it, the classroom teacher knows more than anyone else about the situation that exists in his or her classroom. They are experts on this score."

Concentrated technical education can be a stressful experience for students as well as teachers. Trainers therefore must use a *sense of humor* as an effective tool for easing tension and keeping the program operating smoothly. This observation does not mean that computer educators should aspire to be comedians; however, a pleasant sense of the comical may be a valuable asset.

Another important personal characteristic is the ability to be *directive* when necessary. The effective instructors had enough forcefulness to be able to pull a group of people together and impose some order when large amounts of technical information had to be conveyed.

Instructors also benefit from flexibility and creativity, two traits that proved to be especially useful during the computer institute. Something unexpected happened almost every day during the summer, despite the instructors' thorough planning. Part of the success of the programs was derived from the *flexibility* shown by the instructors. Because of the complexity of technology, one must anticipate that the unexpected will occur in any computer education program. Thus, an effective computer educator should be able to adapt to expecting the unexpected.

Part of the ability to adapt to unexpected circumstances derives from a person's *creativity*. Even beyond that, creativity is important in computer education because there are so few models for planning computer inservice training. Many of the effective presentations we observed were created by the instructors themselves. Similarly, the instructors developed many of their own materials. We imagine this situation will continue in the foreseeable future.

Finally, the best instructors showed an active curiosity about how well the program was doing. Their *tendency to evaluate* seemed to help them make improvements and adjustments as the inservice continued. The instructors planned for evaluation from the outset and were extremely interested in the kinds of feedback they might get from the participants.

SUMMARY

This chapter has described the intensive training program for teacher-trainers conducted by ETS staff, and the 12, month-long summer institutes that were subsequently conducted for educators from the 89 participating secondary schools. Teachers' evaluations of the training programs were presented and the common characteristics of the institutes that we considered to be most effective were identified. Chapter 5 discusses the network support that was provided to the TTIs and high schools, and describes the program in operation.

5 Network Support and Program Operations

Randy Elliot Bennett

The IBM Secondary School Computer Education Program differed from previous vendor-donation programs in several ways. Among the more important differences were the size of the donation, the emphasis on using computers throughout the curriculum, and the requirement that computers be kept together in a laboratory configuration. One other significant factor stands out: the program's commitment to an ongoing technical support network.

This concept called for the grouping of schools into geographically proximal clusters, or networks, and for assigning a teacher-training institution to each network. The expected result of this arrangement was that school staff members would turn to their teacher-training institution (TTI) and to other teachers in their network for support. The 12 networks themselves were in turn to be supported by ETS and IBM.

This chapter describes the network support component of the IBM Secondary School Computer Education Program and, through that component, the program's operation. The bulk of the discussion is devoted to ETS network support, as this is the support function we were most directly involved in. However, an overview of the functions performed by the TTIs in supporting their network schools is also presented, as is a description of the role of IBM technical staff in the program.

ETS NETWORK SUPPORT

The network support activities undertaken by ETS were intended to serve three major purposes. First, activities were designed to assist the TTIs in promoting effective computer use in their schools. Second, these activities were meant to establish and maintain the exchange of information among project participants. Finally, through the assistance and information-exchange processes, network support activities were planned for documenting the operation of the IBM program. To achieve these ends, four complementary activities were undertaken: communications, site visits, midyear meetings, and reports.

Communications

To facilitate the exchange of information among all program participants, several communication mechanisms were established. These mechanisms included telephone contact, a computer-to-computer communications network, and a project newsletter.

Telephone Contact. The first mechanism, telephone contact, facilitated communication between ETS and all project participants. In the early phases of the project, telephone contacts were made by directly calling one of the ETS staff members assigned to the project. Because we anticipated a steady volume of calls throughout the life of the project, a telephone line with an 800 number was installed. This number became operational in late July 1983. The number was made available to TTI staff and to the principal of each school participating in the program. Principals were instructed to call the number if they were unable to get a problem resolved through their TTI.

Between September and the first of December, several dozen calls were logged from TTI staff and from school staff who could not reach their TTI representative or get needed information from that source. Calls from TTI staff overwhelmingly focused on software and hardware and on telecomputing issues. With respect to software and hardware, the most frequently asked questions related to what was being donated and when those products were to arrive. Further, information was often requested on how software provided through the donation program could be obtained. Telecomputing questions mostly centered on how to operate the modem and sign-on to the information utility used by the program.

Computer-to-Computer Communications. Telecomputing capabilities in the IBM Program were provided through donations from the Source Telecomputing Corporation (STC), Tymnet, Inc., and Hayes Microcomputer Products, Inc. Respectively, these vendors provided use of the Source information utility, access to the utility via a long-distance network, and telecommunications hardware and software. In accepting the STC and Tymnet portions of the donation, school staff agreed to: (a) control the school's password, so students did not sign-on to the utility without supervi-

5. NETWORK SUPPORT AND PROGRAM OPERATIONS   65

sion; (b) use the Source for activities other than programming; and (c) ensure that no objectionable material was placed on the Source, and that the privacy of other subscribers and the security of the Source were not harmed.

The use of the Source for exchanging program information was accomplished through SourceMail, an electronic mail service of the information utility. SourceMail permitted the rapid exchange of information between ETS and the TTIs, among the TTIs, and among the schools. Memoranda could be sent to all TTIs at the touch of a button, thus avoiding the time delays encountered in the U.S. Mail and in the repeated phone calls often necessary to catch a busy administrator in the office.

To give TTI staff a chance to learn to use the Source and SourceMail, in particular, accounts were issued to the TTIs first. The earliest communications from TTIs were received around August 31, 1983. All TTIs were not using the Source, however, until late November. The 3-month delay between the earliest sign-on and the establishment of telecomputing capability for all the TTIs was caused by several factors. These included differential access to the necessary hardware and software (some TTIs were able to use their own facilities to sign-on before donated hardware and software arrived) and the different levels of familiarity with telecomputing. The last TTI to receive telecomputing capability had been delayed by the refusal of its legal counsel to approve the terms of the agreement offered by the Source. Unfortunately, this bureaucratic tangle also delayed distribution of Source contracts to the schools in that network.

Between ETS and the networks, SourceMail was used for a variety of communications. First and most important, SourceMail took over the support role previously played by the 800 telephone number. By late November, when most TTIs had begun actively using SourceMail, phone calls to ETS virtually ceased.

In all, several hundred messages were received from TTIs during the school year. The most frequent topics were the Source itself, planning for future meetings, software, and site visits. Messages related to the Source included questions on how to use different facilities, obtain additional free time, renew accounts beyond the period of the donation, and deal with erroneous bills. Communications about future meetings focused on agenda and accommodations. Software questions centered on discounts offered by third party vendors and the procedures for obtaining those reductions, and on the ordering and shipment of IBM-donated software. Finally, site-visit messages most often inquired about the preferred times and places for visits.

Aside from replacing the telephone as the vehicle for responding to questions posed by TTI staff, SourceMail was used to issue bulletins describing the discounts offered program participants by various vendors, to request material for the program newsletter, to broadcast software donations arranged by ETS with third-party vendors, and to schedule visits to program sites. SourceMail, therefore, also largely replaced our use of the U.S. Mail, which had been employed with some frequency to send memoranda and other communications that could not be readily transmitted by telephone.

Introducing high schools to the Source unfortunately took substantially more time to accomplish than introducing TTIs to it did. As late as February, 1984, 12 schools still had not opened their Source accounts, and only half of the 89 schools in the program had ever signed onto the utility. By the following month, however, the vast majority of schools had signed onto the Source at least once, and by May all except one school had logged at least an hour of Source time.

Several difficulties accounted for the delay in getting high schools to use the Source. First, delays arose from the contract-signing procedure. Source contracts were distributed through the TTIs, a procedure that, like software distribution, was designed to strengthen the position of the TTI as the hub of network activity. However, as was true of many other things, the networks accomplished this task with differing degrees of speed and accuracy. Some contracts were lost, some were submitted in duplicate, and some were delayed because of the excessive time taken by one TTI to agree to the terms of the contract with STC.

The second major stumbling block for many schools appeared to be finding a telephone near the computer lab. Most schools had taken their equipment donation to establish a computer laboratory in a classroom. Because classrooms are not routinely wired for telephones, most school principals had to request the installation of a telephone line through their district offices. Like many facilities requests in the schools, installing a telephone line typically took several weeks or months to be acted on.

The final impediment in using telecomputing had to do with perceptions of the activity's potential value. Many school administrators hesitated to involve their students in telecomputing because they feared that the capability might be abused. Some teachers were likewise hesitant because they did not envisage any immediate application of telecomputing to their subject-matter area.

Once up and running, however, telecomputing capabilities were used by several schools in interesting and innovative ways. At least two schools obtained bulletin-board software and operated message services that displayed school and community news and events. In one of these schools, students were given the responsibility of generating new bulletin-board services and writing the program code necessary to make the bulletin board perform those functions. In other schools, the Source was used as a supplement to instruction. The Source's financial-analysis capabilities were applied in teaching a course on the stock market, and the UPI news wire was employed to keep abreast of current events. Finally, students in two New York schools used the electronic mail system to exchange the BASIC subroutines they had written so that programs could be collaboratively developed.

5. NETWORK SUPPORT AND PROGRAM OPERATIONS   67

Program Newsletter. The purpose of the newsletter, *PC Learning,* was to provide participants with information about the operation of the program. The first issue, published in October 1983, contained articles describing the program, the IBM Personal Computer, and the uses of the PC in secondary education. A listing of program participants and of those who donated software and hardware to the project was also included. This first issue gave TTI and school staff an overview from which they could gain a better understanding of the program. In addition, the document could be used to explain the program to others: colleagues, prospective hardware and software donors, friends, and family.

The first issue of the newsletter was written entirely by ETS staff. Because the first issue was meant to provide an overview of the program and an orientation to it, the heavy emphasis on ETS-produced material was necessary. The newsletter's second issue, published in January 1984, took a different direction. This issue introduced a *Network News* column containing reports submitted from several schools and TTIs. In addition, two articles written by TTI staff were included. One of these articles dealt with issues related to minority and female access to computer education programs; the other described innovative teaching uses of the IBM PC in network schools. In all, about half the newsletter's content was contributed by TTI and high school personnel.

The third and fourth newsletters were composed almost entirely of material submitted by program participants. This trend toward incorporating greater amounts of TTI and high school staff contributions was consistent with the philosophy of having the newsletter belong to the program participants, and not to ETS or IBM.

Press runs for each issue of *PC Learning* totaled about 5,000 copies. Classroom sets of each issue were distributed to each school and TTI, the IBM technical representatives, and the IBM project officer. Individual copies were sent to each participating school principal, to the major computing periodicals, and to a small list of persons who had displayed interest in the program.

Site Visits

Visits to the TTIs and high schools constituted ETS's second major network support activity. Site visits were initiated during the summer, when training of high school staff was underway, and continued over the school year.

Site visits were conducted for several reasons consistent with the general purpose of network support. Visits to program sites allowed TTI and high school staff to discuss problems directly with ETS staff. For example, during one of the early visits, it was discovered that the staff of one TTI was unsure about whether their institution was going to compensate them for time spent delivering summer training to high school teachers. Because such a lack of administrative support did not bode well for the future functioning of that network, the problem was taken up by the site visitor with the TTI administrator on the same day it was reported. The administrator was offered assistance in dealing with those organization managers responsible for approving compensation. Although the question could not be resolved that day, visiting the site resulted in identifying the problem and initiating action toward an eventual solution.

Besides pinpointing problems, site visits served to document the implementation of the program. Visits allowed ETS staff to view the physical facilities in which machines were placed, sample the activities engaged in by students, and meet the staff responsible for coordinating computer-education efforts. The visits permitted detailed understanding of the program's operation that would not have otherwise been possible.

The final purpose of conducting site visits was to facilitate the exchange of information among the 12 networks. In ETS's visits to individual schools, interests were inevitably expressed and questions raised by one teacher that corresponded to the work of a teacher in another network. By visiting a variety of sites, ETS staff could begin to develop an informal catalog of information about who was interested in what types of application. Referrals of one teacher or network trainer to another could then be made, with subsequent contact initiated through either SourceMail or conventional communications methods.

As has been mentioned, site visits were first undertaken during the summer, when high school teachers were being trained by the TTI staff, and continued during the school year, when the program was being carried out in the high schools. During the summer, 26 visits were made, including at least one visit to each of the 12 TTIs. Multiple visits were made to some TTIs to increase the reliability of observations, observe training sessions that had been split into early and late summer segments, and assist in those instances where difficulties had been discovered on the first visit. In one unusual case, a TTI was visited repeatedly, because training was going extraordinarily well. The techniques used at this TTI seemd so worthy and the instructors and participating teachers so enthusiastic that thorough documentation of the TTI's summer program was considered essential. ETS staff decided, therefore, that a case study of the training experience should be written (Stecher, 1984b) in the hope that the record would prove valuable to others interested in elements contributing to successful staff development programs.

In all, 6 of the 12 TTIs were visited more than once during the summer training. One TTI was visited seven times (to develop the case study), three were visited three times, and two were visited twice. Impressions about TTI training, gleaned from these visits, are presented in the preceding chapter on training.

After summer training, several TTIs were visited on days when network meetings were held. These visits were made to assess the school staff mem-

5. NETWORK SUPPORT AND PROGRAM OPERATIONS   69

bers' need for continuing support and the network's success in responding to that need. Visits by ETS to the high schools did not begin until early December and continued periodically through April 1984. High school visits began later in the year because ETS and IBM staff thought that school personnel should be given a chance to get the programs organized before having to display their accomplishments to outsiders.

In all, 57 of the 89 program schools were visited during the academic year. Of these 57 schools, 10 were visited a second time before the conclusion of the program. The number of schools visited in each network varied from three to seven. Most site visits were a half day long and included the following: (a) examination of the physical facilities; (b) observation of students using the computer lab; (c) meetings with the computer-education coordinator, subject-matter teachers working with the machines, and the principal or other school administrator; and (d) collection of various documents about the school's computer-education program (e.g., class schedules, lab regulations, lesson plans and exercises, and student programs and their outputs).

Several methods were used to document the results of site visits. For visits made early in the program, observers recorded their impressions in narrative reports. Later visits were documented through a pair of questionnaires filled out by both the site visitor and a school-staff representative.

From a review of site-visit reports, questionnaires, and documents collected during the visits, we can offer some impressions about the operation of the IBM program during this period. These impressions are of how donated computers were used, how much they were used, and how they were physically organized and maintained. Other variables, particularly the expenses incurred by schools in running the program, are discussed in other chapters of this volume.

In considering ETS's perceptions of the program's operation, one must keep in mind that site visits spanned a period of several months during which the program was undergoing substantial formative change. Those sites visited in early December might well have changed significantly by the time site visits were completed in April. Similarly, those sites visited later in the winter might have taken on a far different character by the close of the school year.

Visits to schools revealed great variety in the ways donated computers were being used. In general, computers were being used in four primary contexts. The first of these contexts was the high school course. Courses using computers were of two types: those that focused upon the computer as the subject of instruction and those that adopted the computer as a supplement to instruction in another content area. Courses in the former category centered primarily on introducing the computer or on teaching programming. Students enrolled in introductory courses learned basic computer-literacy skills that often included computer assisted instruction (CAI) on the PC's disk operating system, keyboard skills, and a sampling of applications packages such as a wordprocessor, a database manager, and a spreadsheet. Those taking programming courses seemed most often to learn BASIC, though some courses were observed using Pascal (often in preparation for the College Board's Computer Science Advanced Placement Examination) and Fortran.

Within the context of the high-school course, computers were also employed as supplements in a wide variety of classes that focused on some subject matter other than the computer. Among these courses were English, remedial writing, Spanish, religion, social studies, accounting, physics, biology, earth science, chemistry, marine biology, mathematics, special education, technical drawing, art, physical education, home economics, business education, and history. The most popular use within this course domain appeared to be word processing. Word processing was most commonly used in English classes to produce essays, journals, newspapers, and pieces of creative writing; in business classes as a basic secretarial tool; and in other humanities and science courses for preparing reports and compositions.

Another common application of the computers in subject-matter classes was data aggregation and presentation. For example, at one school the physics teacher divided class time among lectures, demonstrations, and lab work. For lab work, students were organized into teams of three each. Teams were responsible for conducting their experiments and then reporting to the computer lab where they could aggregate and summarize their results, using Multiplan. At another school, PFS: File was employed to help physical education students monitor changes in body functions. Blood-pressure and heart-rate measurements were taken over the course of the semester, and changes in these indices were displayed with PFS: Graph.

A third, though apparently less common, supplementary activity involved planning. In this category, spreadsheets were used by college-bound seniors learning about personal finance. With VisiCalc, these students developed expense budgets for their freshman year and a register for recording checking account transactions. At another school, special education students employed Multiplan in the process of learning how to develop a grocery budget.

Finally, CAI was occasionally observed in subject-matter classes. Because many teachers expressed interest in CAI software, we must conclude that the apparent lack of CAI use was due more to the dearth of CAI programs for the IBM PC than to teacher intention. Of the few CAI applications that were observed, one of the more popular was preparing students for college admissions tests.

Of the two uses of computers in high school courses—that is, as subject of and supplement to instruction—the IBM program emphasized the latter use. Even so, observations made during our site visits suggested that many participating schools devoted substantial time to coursework in computer programming and literacy, work that is rapidly becoming an accepted part of the standard high-school curriculum. Hence, we came to see such use as a legitimate application of computers to a curriculum area, though not the broader use that had been originally envisioned.

5. NETWORK SUPPORT AND PROGRAM OPERATIONS

In addition to the high school course, computers were used by many schools in the context of computer clubs and other student organizations. Such groups ran the gamut from informal affairs — distinguished only by the computer lab's being kept open after school hours — to highly organized activities. Of the latter, the most popular appeared to center on school publications. In particular, many schools used their IBM PCs to help prepare the school newspaper. This task was greatly simplified by EasyWriter's ability to print column formats and by the availability of software for producing type sizes suitable for headlines. One school was even able to produce a trilingual newspaper, though accent marks needed to be added manually.

The third major context in which computers were used was inservice training for teachers not in the summer training program. Inservice efforts varied from no program to extensive multiweek efforts. At one group of Florida schools, inservice activities consisted of 15 weekly 2-hour sessions. At another school, the only program was to allow teachers to check out machines on school holidays. Ironically, principals in several schools having no organized programs commented that teacher interest in the machines was so great that inservice activities would only create a demand for machine time that could not possibly be fulfilled.

Inservice instruction was most often provided by teachers trained through the local TTI. Those trained were themselves almost exclusively teachers; only a few cases were noted in which administrators or board members participated. Attendees sometimes received compensation, most often credit toward advancement on the district salary scale. In at least one case, however, teachers interested in learning about computers enrolled in courses offered through the school's adult education program and were charged a nominal fee for the privilege.

Teachers' interest in joining inservice activities appeared surprisingly high. In one California school, a week-long session was offered at the beginning of the year to 60 out of 100 faculty members. At a New York school, more than 90 teachers were trained. Interest at some schools was so great that regular student use of the machines had to be postponed a semester while teacher demand was being satisfied.

Content covered at inservice sessions varied across schools. In one school, a single application, word processing, was emphasized to show teachers how they could use the computer immediately for their own work. Combined with the purchase of a letter-quality printer and the easy-to-learn PFS: Write word-processing package, this strategy proved very successful. At other schools, more traditional content was covered, the focus of activity being centered on introductions to the IBM PC hardware and software.

The fourth context for computer use was adult education and other community activities. This use of computers appeared to be largely motivated by a desire to build further support for computer education by involving community members directly in the program. In addition, such activities typically returned a small profit that could be used to help expand computer-education activities. Content covered in adult-education and community-education courses included introductory computer concepts, programming, word processing, and business applications.

An indication of the potential for building community support can be seen from the types of organizations with which schools collaborated in offering extracurricular programs. One upstate New York school offered adult-education programs in collaboration with the local Parks and Recreation Department. Several schools in Florida teamed up with local universities to offer graduate courses, whereas other schools worked with community colleges to provide students with computer-education opportunities.

In addition to the variety of contexts in which computers were used, we observed great variety in the extent of use—from a few periods a week to solidly booked days, evenings, and weekends. Among the factors that discouraged use was many subject-matter teachers' inability to apply the machines to their academic content areas. For these teachers, the time necessary to create ideas, lesson plans, exercises, and data files was simply not available. In addition, the absence of content-specific CAI software for the IBM PC left these teachers with no alternative but to pursue teaching along conventional paths.

In addition to type and extent of use, site visits offered much information on how donated computers were physically deployed and maintained. In accordance with the original program design, virtually all computers were grouped in a centralized lab in every school visited. However, sometimes a machine or two was separated from the group to be placed in a library, school newspaper office, teachers room, or elsewhere.

To take responsibility for laboratory operations, several schools hired a full-time assistant, whose responsibilities included scheduling classes, ordering supplies, cataloging and dispensing software, and arranging for hardware repair. Other schools split these responsibilities among teachers using the lab and a district or building computer-education coordinator. Still others relied on student or parent volunteers to assist with laboratory operations and with supervising students during open lab periods. Finally, teachers were frequently found donating time to keep labs open during lunch periods and after school.

Computer labs were typically protected from robbery and vandalism by a variety of security measures. At the most basic level, many school administrators limited distribution of lab keys to a few select individuals. At some schools, more involved measures were taken: reinforced doors and pickproof locks were installed at lab entrances; false ceilings were removed so barriers could be placed above walls to prevent entry from adjoining rooms; and machines were secured to furniture through homemade or commercially available locking systems. A few schools even installed sophisticated burglar alarms. That schools—including those in low-crime areas—went to the expense and trouble to take such extensive measures is notable: It suggests the high value school administrators placed on the IBM donation.

Maintenance of computer lab equipment was most commonly handled on an ad hoc basis, without benefit of any long-term service arrangement. In this case, malfunctioning equipment was brought to the vendor of choice (e.g., Computerland, IBM, TRW) for repair charged at an hourly rate. As an alternative, several networks established consortia arrangements whereby the TTI provided repair service at below-market prices in return for an annual membership fee. Finally, some schools purchased maintenance agreements from IBM or other local vendors.

Fortunately for those with ad hoc maintenance arrangements, the incidence of equipment failure was surprisingly low, especially given the heavy use and difficult environmental conditions that some machines were subjected to (e.g., heavy concentrations of chalk dust). The overwhelming majority of problems occurred at set-up (e.g., incorrect switch settings, defective boards or memory chips) and were promptly corrected under the IBM warranty. Beyond this point, problems were almost completely restricted to disk drive doors, which in isolated instances broke when opened too forcefully. This problem was traced to a batch of disk drives that had been fitted with a plastic door pin no longer used in production. Once replaced, the doors functioned without difficulty.

Midyear Meetings

The third network support activity centered on meetings of ETS, IBM, and TTI staff members. The purpose of these meetings was to exchange information about the progress of the program. Two meetings were held: one in San Jose from November 1 through 3 and one in Atlanta from March 6 through 8.

Although the San Jose meeting was held early in the life of the project, in the trainers' view several factors emerged as ultimately influencing the success of the program. Among the most important of these factors were limited preparation time and administrative support. Almost without exception, trainers agreed that the program was hindered by the curtailed amount of time available for start-up activities. TTI staff members had been asked, in the space of weeks, to learn to operate a machine completely unfamiliar to them, become proficient at several applications packages, develop a plan for training teachers from their network schools, and set up their computer laboratories. Across TTIs, the average time between leaving Princeton and starting teacher training was approximately 5 ½ weeks. In Polk County, trainers had only 2 weeks to prepare before high school teachers began arriving at the TTI for summer instruction. This limited time understandably restricted the type, number, and quality of instructional lessons that could be prepared.

TTI trainers reported that the insufficient preparation time also affected high school teachers. Like the trainers, teachers had to learn to operate the machine, become familiar with several applications packages, plan lessons, set up computer labs, and schedule classes. In the *best* case, teachers completed their 4-week training course at the end of July, leaving between 2 and 6 weeks—depending on the scheduled opening of school—for preparation. Time problems were further compounded by many teachers having planned well-deserved vacations, which they were most reluctant to reschedule. Given these limitations, it was a wonder that any use of the computers during the fall semester was made at all.

A second factor, unanimously cited by those attending the San Jose meeting as a critical influence on the success of the program, was administrative support. Attendees agreed that strong commitments from school principals and district superintendents were essential for the program's success. Attendees felt that success in any given school would be seriously jeopardized if administrators did not make the strongest possible commitment to supporting the program. In fact, there was agreement that a specific written guarantee of support be required as a precondition for participation in any future programs.

The main type of administrative support deemed so crucial to success was financial. Money was needed to pay teachers for time spent in summer training and in preparing lessons for use in the fall. Funds were needed for substitutes who could stand in during the year while regular teachers attended network meetings, developed curricular and instructional materials, and learned new software. Money was needed to set up a computer education lab. Physical space had to be acquired; furniture located, purchased, or specially constructed; rooms rewired; and security systems and telephone lines installed. Finally, money was needed for new software, supplies, and equipment maintenance. Though a substantial amount of software was donated through the program, there would still be much software to purchase if teachers were to have available those packages most relevant to their own instructional content areas. Similarly, blank diskettes for use by students would have to be obtained, as would printer paper and ribbons. Money would also have to be set aside for fixing equipment when it broke down.

After only a few months' experience with program schools, many attendees found district administrators unwilling to commit funds toward released time for teachers to attend network meetings or toward the maintenance of the donated equipment. TTI trainers were discouraged by this attitude, for many felt that their own efforts were wasted without the full support of school administrators.

In addition to factors affecting the success of the program, attendees at the San Jose meeting offered information about other aspects of the program's progress. According to the trainers, word-processing programs were receiving the most widespread use in project schools, and spreadsheets were receiving the least attention. Second, the program's focus on using generic software, such as word processors and spreadsheets, was reported to be troubling to some teachers who could not readily apply these packages to their curricula. Many teachers desired CAI packages that could be used with little preparation to teach students. Finally, attendees expressed some disappointment in the list of software that had been offered to schools through the program. The list was perceived by trainers as placing too much emphasis on programming tools (e.g., compilers, assemblers, and program-development utilities) and not enough on instructional courseware and applications packages.

Because of its timing, the San Jose meeting was necessarily limited to discussing early reactions. In contrast, those attending the Atlanta meeting in March had the benefit of the greater part of the school year to formulate judgments about the program's operation. In the opinion of TTI staff, several strengths characterized the program. Among these were the inclusion of disciplines other than math and science in the program, the program's emphasis on staff development, the sharing that took place among project participants, and the quality of the hardware and initial software donations. In addition, an increase in enthusiasm among both students and teachers was attributed to the program.

The topic of greatest concern to TTI staff was IBM's intention to terminate support for the project at the end of June. Participants strongly felt that the program should continue in some form. At a minimum, TTI staff believed it important to establish a mechanism for maintaining contact among themselves. Also deemed critical was the sharing of lessons learned from the current program with schools taking part in IBM's future computer-education efforts.

A second important concern was the program's emphasis on using the computer as a tool in various subject-matter areas. As in the previous meeting, TTI staff believed that nontrivial uses of the computer in many subject areas outside of science, mathematics, and business were difficult for teachers to find. In combination, the limited practical utility of the tool concept and the concurrent lack of CAI courseware for the IBM Personal Computer were keeping many teachers in the nontechnical disciplines from incorporating the machines into their courses.

The limited use of telecomputing made by the high schools constituted a third serious concern of the group. As noted, the problems impeding use of the Source included both the cost and red tape involved in installing phone lines and the administrators' fears of student abuse of telecomputing capability. Several TTI staff added their belief that the services offered by the Source were of little direct relevance to the secondary school curriculum. Hence, many teachers felt little incentive to use the information utility with their students.

The final shared concerns were again time and administrative support. These concerns had been perceived early in the program and received attention at the San Jose meeting. Their re-emergence in Atlanta suggested that these factors still hampered the success of the program. Given their already full load of responsibilities, many teachers still could not find the time to plan lessons, run a lab, and review new software. Many administrators also could not or would not make release time available for these activities, or provide other support to the program.

Apart from substance, the Atlanta meeting differed from the San Jose meeting in the manner in which it was planned and administered. The San Jose meeting was planned and chaired by ETS staff. Although the meeting was productive, the discussion followed lines that ETS staff felt were important to the progress of the program. During that meeting, several TTI staff indicated an interest in having greater input into the agenda for the next meeting. Consequently, a committee of TTI personnel was established to plan and chair the Atlanta meeting. This arrangement produced a sense of ownership and interest at the meeting that had not been as apparent at the earlier get-together. The result was a more productive, interactive, and positive meeting.

Reports

The fourth and final network support activity was the production of interim and final reports. The purpose of these was to help in documenting what had occurred throughout the 12 networks composing the program. In late October, ETS project staff asked TTI coordinators to submit a first report that was to describe the process of setting up the operation of the TTI, the summer training, and the delivery and installation of machines in network schools. It was emphasized to TTI coordinators that the specific content, format, and length of the report was open and should be based on the best judgments of TTI staff members.

The letter containing this information also asked TTI coordinators to be prepared to submit two additional reports. One of these, due in January, was to describe how computers were being used in the high schools during the fall semester and what activities had been undertaken by the TTI to support the network schools. The final report would describe network activities taking place during the spring and recap the events of the school year.

In response to our request for documentation of the initial stages of the project, 11 of the 12 TTIs submitted reports. Six were received by February, and the remainder were submitted later in the school year. Formats ranged from a page or two of text and some appendices containing letters and meeting agenda, to one finely crafted, 60-page narrative detailing all elements of TTI training.

5. NETWORK SUPPORT AND PROGRAM OPERATIONS   77

The questions suggested by ETS staff for completing the first report focused on TTI training. Information gathered on this topic has already been discussed in chapter 4. However, because five of the reports were produced and submitted later in the school year, information on the functioning of the program in the network schools was often included. In general, this information supported and extended observations made during site visits, especially those concerning the use of machines in various contexts, frequency of use, and equipment organization.

Tables 5.1 and 5.2 present a list of events and an analysis of the number of students using IBM PCs at Tioga Central High School in New York. As the tables suggest, machines were being employed in the four contexts identified through site visits: courses, teacher inservice education, after-school student activities, and adult and community continuing education. Of particular note with respect to the last category is the course offering, "The PC and Office Practices," for employees of a local business (see the Oct. 18, 1983, entry in Table 5.1). Developing relationships with the local business community would appear to be a critical step in opening avenues for student internship and job placement, and in extending the base of support for school activities.

At American High School in Florida the use of the IBM lab for adult and community education included biweekly meetings of the local IBM PC User's Group, weekly sessions of a Florida International University course, and meetings of the Parents' Computer Booster Club. American's student club activities centered on the Patriot Processors, a group of students doing word processing for teachers and students.

The following quotations are from teachers who had completed inservice training at Florida's Coral Gables High School (Bernard, 1984). As they suggest, donated computers were beginning to be used in yet another context. This context is classroom administration. From these quotations it is clear that several teachers saw the computer as a time-saving tool for making tests, keeping records, and writing lesson plans and memos.

> Yesterday at an area guidance meeting we learned that a project is underway to set up information retrieval programs which will necessitate the (use of computer) terminals by counselors...I felt none of the panic some of the others exhibited.
> —Guidance Counselor

> The world of computers is no longer...an alien one. I see all kinds of applications for my teaching. I'm going to (buy) one!
> —English Teacher

> ...Now I realize how I could use a personal computer as a teacher to make tests, keep records and memos.
> —Science Teacher

TABLE 5.1
Time Line of Tioga Central H.S. Computer Events

SEPT. 2 1983	– IBM PC's delivered
SEPT. 6 1983	– District wide faculty presentation on the IBM Secondary Schools Program.
	High school presentation on the computer inservice program and availability of computer time.
SEPT. 7 1983	– Distribution to each department of courseware material created at the teacher training institute.
	Beginning of a BASIC programming course 3rd and 4th periods five days a week.
SEPT. 9 1983	– IBM PC's installed.
	Introduction of math 7 (one) to the IBM PC's.
SEPT. 12 1983	– Programming students began putting DOS on programs and making backups.
SEPT. 14 1983	– Introduction of high school history class to the IBM PC.
SEPT. 15 1983	– Introduction of another high school history class to the IBM PC.
	Opening of the computer room one-half hour before the start of school.
	Opening of the computer room 1 hour after school.
SEPT. 19 1983	– Introduction of math 7 (two) to the IBM PC's.
SEPT. 20 1983	– Beginning of a word processing course 2nd period two days a week for 10 weeks.
OCT. 3 1983	– Introduction of a fourth grade class to the IBM PC.
OCT. 5 1983	– Presentation and introduction to the school board on the IBM PC's and the IBM secondary schools program.
OCT. 11 1983	– Beginning of a six-week inservice course for high school teachers on the IBM PC.
OCT. 17 1983	– Beginning of a six-week "Introduction to Computers" course for the continuing education program.
OCT. 18 1983	– Beginning of a six-week "The PC and Office Practices" course for employees of Ellis-Edson–Beaudry Inc.
NOV. 4 1983	– Set up the Hayes modem.
NOV. 8 1983	– PC and Easywriter being used in the shorthand and transcription class.

5. NETWORK SUPPORT AND PROGRAM OPERATIONS

TABLE 5.1 *(continued)*

NOV. 15 1983	– District-wide open house and computer demonstration.
DEC. 5 1983	– Beginning of the PC and PFS: File being used in eighth grade language arts.
DEC. 6 1983	– Host for the TTI schools and demonstration of telecommunications.
DEC. 7 1983	– Adult education course – introduction to computers taught by Mrs. Dodge.
JAN. 4 1984	– Beginning of a computer workshop for elementary school staff.
JAN. 5 1984	– Beginning of a computer workshop for middle school staff.
JAN. 9 1984	– Adult education course – "The PC and Office Practices."
JAN. 10 1984	– Adult education course – "Introduction to Computers" taught by Mrs. Baxter.
JAN. 10 1984	– Starting to use the Hayes modem and the Source.
JAN. 11 1984	– PC and Easywriter being used in English 11 class.
JAN. 30 1984	– Beginning of advanced programming course for upper classmen.
JAN. 30 1984	– Beginning of computer literacy course.
FEB. 1 1984	– Adult education – "Programming and the PC" taught by Mrs. Dodge.
FEB. 23 1984	– Adult education – "Introduction to Computers" taught by Mr. Crotsley.
MAR. 23 1984	– Changed system configuration to include the printer and modem in one system.

Source: Tioga Central High School. (March, 1984). *IBM Secondary Schools Project: Vital Statistics.* Tioga Center, NY: Author. Used by permission.

I have found my instruction improved due to the use of the IBM PC. I have come up during my planning periods at least six times in February to print out tests, lesson plans...The computer has motivated me to do more because of its ease over the typewriter.

— Phys. Ed. Teacher

... The reality of the lab being available to me, on my planning period, for example, to type tests...that I may reuse from year-to-year is exciting!

— Debate Coach

This...is fantastic! I can see how it is beneficial, in saving time and energy, in practically any profession...

— English Teacher

TABLE 5.2
Tioga Central H.S. Computer Course Enrollments

Course	Enrollment
High school inservice workshop	15
Middle school computer workshop	14
Elementary school computer workshop	12
Total staff	41
BASIC programming I – Soph., Jr., Sr.	36
BASIC programming II – Soph., Jr., Sr.	36
Computer literacy – Jr., Sr.	30
Shorthand & transcription	12
Total student	114
Language arts – 8th grade	29
English 11	16
Math 7	110
Total student	155
Continuing education:	
Introduction to Computers	90
Programming in BASIC	12
Introduction to Computers – scheduled for course	45
Total adults	147

Source: Tioga Central High School. (March, 1984). *IBM Secondary Schools Project: Vital Statistics.* Tioga Center, NY: Author. Used by permission.

In addition to use *across* a variety of contexts, the interim reports suggest that the computers were being frequently used *within* these contexts. In particular, inservice training activities appeared to be widespread. For example, the reports indicated that all schools in the San Jose and Polk County networks had conducted, or were in the process of implementing, some type of professional development program.

As suggested by the site visits, use of the machines in student courses also appeared to be extensive and varied. In the San Jose network alone, computers were reportedly used in English, journalism, literature, Spanish, U.S. history, world history, social studies, physiology, biology, architectural and technical drawing, mathematics, introduction to computers, computer literacy, introduction to BASIC, intermediate BASIC programming, advanced

5. NETWORK SUPPORT AND PROGRAM OPERATIONS

programming, Advanced Placement computer mathematics, word processing, and typing (Anderson, undated). A similar degree of diversity was evident in the Vassar College network.

From the listing of the titles previously presented, it is clear that computers were used in subject-matter as well as literacy and programming courses. In subject-matter areas such as the liberal arts and the social and physical sciences, computers were most commonly employed for word processing. As might be expected, a greater variety of applications programs were used in the literacy courses, including language and operating system tutorials, database managers, word processors, and occasionally, spreadsheet and drawing programs. Programming courses used tutorials and language compilers and interpreters.

The interim reports also added interesting information to our perspective on equipment organization, especially lab staffing. In particular, the reports suggested that parents were contributing significant amounts of time as aides, curriculum consultants, and programmers in several schools. Along with the establishment of adult-education and community-education courses, this type of active parent involvement implied a growing interaction between the school and community, one which could only serve to strengthen computer-education programs.

Although the interim reports added valuable insight to our understanding of the operation of the IBM program, the low response rate for the first interim report suggested that little was to be gained from requesting additional written documentation from the TTIs. It was therefore decided that, in lieu of further reports, data for program documentation would be gathered by ETS staff through a telephone interview with TTI trainers and coordinators. These interviews, conducted after the close of the IBM program, provided a clearer picture of the network support efforts expended by TTI and IBM representatives.

TTI NETWORK SUPPORT

As has been stated, the primary mission of each TTI was to support the schools belonging to its local network. What kinds of activities were conducted by TTI personnel under these auspices? An indication of the type of support provided by the TTIs comes from the interviews with TTI staff and from several of the interim reports.

From a review of these data sources, TTI support can be placed into three categories: group meetings, individual assistance, and general communications. Group meetings were held on a regular basis in all networks. In several networks, meeting locations were rotated to give school staff members the opportunity to see lab arrangements in their sister schools (see Table 5.3 for

TABLE 5.3
Network Meetings for One TTI

Date	Place	Attendance (includes TTI-staff)	Activities
Sept. 21, 1983	San Jose State	13	Administrators meeting. Intros, sharing, problem-solving, hands-on w/PCs
Oct. 7, 1983	Blackford High	8 from SJSU-TTI	Joint-meeting w/County Office TTI-Network & ETS. Intros, sharing & discussion. Source intro.
Oct. 25, 1983	Institute of Computer Technology (Instructor: Kevin Terrill)	11	Special equipment maintenance workshop for coordinators/technicians
Oct. 26, 1983	Overfelt High	17	Intros, individual school overviews, tour of *all* computer labs, modem demonstration, problem solving, slides of training workshop, problem solving, materials packet
Nov. 29, 1983	California School for the Deaf	15	Tour, sharing, materials review, discussion, Source review and demonstration materials packet distrbt.w/SCOM dsk
Jan. 24, 1984	Bellarmine	10	Curriculum development using decision-making problem-solving, and creativity models & activities w/hardouts, PC lab tour.
Mar. 15, 1984	Pioneer High (Speaker: Brian Stecher, ETS) (Guest: Patti Warren, IBM)	29	Luncheon, PC lab tour & demonstrations, speaker followed by questions/answers, materials packet
May 4, 1984	San Jose State (Speaker: Judy Powers, COE) (Demonstration: Charles Berry) (Mission Computers)	10	Speaker from COE Microcomputer center sharing/discussion, 1984–85 planning, demonstration of software and IBM-PC jr.

Source: Anderson, E. S. (undated). *IBM*: *TTI-Coordinator's summary report: IBM Secondary Schools Program 1983–84*. San Jose, CA, San Jose State University. Used by permission.

5. NETWORK SUPPORT AND PROGRAM OPERATIONS 83

one example). In other networks, meetings were primarily held at the TTI. Attendance at meetings seemed to vary within and across networks, several members from a school attending on some occasions and one representative per school on others.

The content of meetings varied from formal workshops and demonstrations to informal discussion and review sessions (see Table 5.3). Workshops were offered on such topics as communications and equipment maintenance; demonstrations of plotters, voice synthesizers, and other peripherals were provided. Informal sessions involved discussion of problems encountered in each school and individual review of new software packages. At some meetings, programs developed by teachers, students, and other public-domain producers were exchanged.

Individual assistance constituted the second type of support given by TTIs. Such assistance centered primarily on hardware and software issues, though curriculum and administrative support problems were also dealt with. Advice was given on equipment purchases (e.g., double-sided disk drives, letter quality printers, additional memory), set-up (particularly communications equipment), operation, and repair (e.g., diagnosing problems, obtaining parts and service). Consultation on software purchase and operation (again, particularly communications) was also provided.

Assistance included both off-site and on-site consultation. Off-site consultation was provided by telephone or by computer-to-computer communications. Three TTIs installed hotlines tied to answering machines that could be called day or night. Two institutions set up their own computer-to-computer communication networks. Vassar used its university computer facility to receive and respond to requests from school personnel, and Queens College used BitNet, a nationwide academic computing network. On-site assistance was provided during the course of scheduled visits by TTI staff to network schools or through ad hoc visits resulting from a special request. The activities conducted onsite included helping school staff members set up and learn to operate communications equipment and diagnose hardware problems.

General communications between TTI and school-staff members were accomplished through several methods. Program newsletters were published by Vassar College, San Jose State University, the Santa Clara Teacher Education and Computer Center, and Florida Atlantic University (FAU). FAU's newsletter was electronically accessed through its bulletin board system. Newsletters announced the dates and content for upcoming meetings, reported on the progress made by network schools in particular areas (e.g., inservice education), and offered computer education tips.

IBM NETWORK SUPPORT

In order to provide another level of technical support to the program, a local IBM representative was assigned to each site, with the exception of the two Los Angeles and two San Jose area TTIs, each of which shared a representative. As specified in the original program design, these persons were meant to function as technical safety nets. TTI staff members were to call the technical representative only when they could not get a problem resolved by ETS. School personnel were to contact these persons only when they encountered an emergency that could not be handled through the TTI or ETS.

To what extent were IBM technical representatives used by the TTI and school personnel? Information on this question comes from interviews conducted after the close of the program with representatives from each TTI and with each of the IBM technical representatives.

From these data sources it is clear that the technical representatives were most heavily involved in the program at the time of initial hardware delivery. Most technical representatives were substantially involved in coordinating machine delivery, set-up, and inventory. Furthermore, they took responsibility for working with TTI and school personnel to resolve early problems encountered with hardware. Once these initial hardware problems were resolved, demand for technical assistance decreased dramatically in most instances.

For the remainder of the program, most of the interviewewd IBM staff members functioned in representative, rather than technical, roles. These roles involved arranging visits to IBM research facilities and setting up demonstrations, securing the donation of supplies (e.g., paper), making TTI and school visits, and providing general encouragement and support. At least two technical representatives devoted significant time to these activities, developing such effective working relationships with TTI and school personnel that they seemed to become regular members of the local network support team. Both of these staffers attended TTI network meetings and routinely visited schools.

When technical assistance was provided by IBM staffers, this assistance involved setting up modems, dealing with occasional hardware problems, providing advice on additional purchases (e.g., large screen projection systems), and responding to questions about the operation of particular software packages.

In summary, the eight IBM technical representatives played key roles in facilitating the hardware installation phase of the project. In addition, several representatives were active in providing ongoing technical advice and assistance.

SUMMARY

In this chapter, we have described the network support activities of ETS, TTI, and IBM staff members. In addition, we have constructed a picture of

5. NETWORK SUPPORT AND PROGRAM OPERATIONS   85

the program's operation on the basis of information gathered through these network support activities. We now turn to a discussion of the costs of computer education at the school level. This discussion offers both a better understanding of the value of the IBM program to the participating schools and an indication of the costs that might be incurred by other schools that establish similar computer-education programs.

6 The Cost of Implementing Computer-Based Education

Brian Stecher

How much does computer-based education cost? School administrators and program developers would love to have a simple answer to this question; however, no simple answer exists. The issue is complicated because there is so much variety in the way schools use computers. Some schools conduct a "computer education" program with one donated microcomputer and a few ditto sheets; others spend great sums of money to equip every classroom with hardware and software, organize extensive inservice training for staff, purchase textbooks and supplemental materials, and so on. Clearly, such differences in the implementation of computer education will affect cost, just as they affect patterns of use (Center for the Social Organization of Schools, 1983b).

Given such variation, one might despair to finding meaningful generalizations about cost. Yet, despite these complications, much can be learned about the cost of computer-based education from an examination of selected programs. The IBM program provided an unusual opportunity to gather comparative information about the resources required to incorporate computers in educational programs. Moreover, it shed some light on the relationships that exist between cost and program characteristics.

The goal of this chapter is to share information about the cost of the IBM program. In particular, the levels of resources that were necessary for effective program implementation and the balance that existed between the costs of hardware, software, site preparation, and staff development are described. In addition, relationships between program characteristics and cost are explored, and a few general principles for linking cost and program characteristics are suggested. Finally, we share some of the fund-raising strategies that participating schools used to raise money to cover local costs. It is our hope that all this information helps program administrators to assess resource needs, review project budgets, and to raise funds for their own computer-education projects.

It is important to understand the meaning of the term *cost* and the procedures that are used in cost analysis to appreciate the information contained in this chapter. Most people equate cost with expenditures and imagine that it is fairly easy to determine how much was spent. However, the complete cost of a program includes more than just the expenditures that appear on a project budget or financial statement. One must consider the value of *all* the elements that are necessary to conduct the project (i.e., all the resources that another school would have to supply in order to duplicate the project). So one must broaden the discussion from "how much was spent?" to "how much was provided?" The following dialogue illustrates this point with an example from computer-based education.

AN ILLUSTRATIVE DIALOGUE

Imagine the following hypothetical scene: Tracy Robinson, principal of El Serano High School, visits a nearby school to observe the computer-education program. Twelve personal computers have been placed in a laboratory that teachers can reserve for one or more class periods. Tracy visits the lab and likes what she sees. She asks the principal:

Q: How much did it cost you to get your computer-education program started?

A: It was a lot cheaper than people think. We spent $2,300 each on the 12 computers and another $1,200 on two printers. So that's only about $29,000.

Q: You're right; that is cheap. But what about all the software?

A: Right. I forgot that. We bought LOGO and Bank Street Writer for about $1,200.

Q: So that's $30,000. What about the lock-down tables I saw?

A: Now that you remind me, we bought those "anchor pads" to secure the computers to the tables. Otherwise we'd have just about zero computers left. That cost us about $2,500.

Q: Did you buy all the textbooks I saw, and the blank disks? That looked like another $1,500 or so to me.

A: No, we were lucky there. I arranged to get a set of BASIC textbooks and workbooks from the Adult School in exchange for using the computers two nights a week. And we got our parent teacher club to donate 250 blank disks, so these didn't cost us anything.

Q: But it would actually cost me a lot more than $30,000 unless I can do a whole lot of finagling.

A: Yes, but you're good at that.

Q: Thank you, I think. By the way, how did you decide which computers to buy?

A: Are you kidding? I spent a whole year planning this program. My computer teacher and I visited other schools, went to conferences, read magazines. I talked to Bank Street on the phone. We really got into it.

Q: So, that was a lot of your time to get started. How much of your time goes into the program now?

A: I don't know. I probably spend 5 to 6 hours a week on this project. I get calls from parents, "Why isn't Johnny or Jimmy using the computer?" I have visitors like you who want to look at what we've accomplished. You know, that sort of thing.

Q: OK. So you put in a lot of your own time. By the way, how did you handle teacher inservice? None of my staff has any background with computers.

A: Well, a couple of the teachers already had computers of their own, so they did a staff development workshop for the rest of the group. Then we got a staff development grant to release the teachers to observe in each other's classrooms. And a couple of teachers enrolled in night classes at State College on their own.

This abbreviated dialogue illustrates many of the complexities that arise in a cost analysis of a computer-based education program. In addition to the major direct expenditures, there are many smaller expenditures that are easily overlooked, as well as many indirect costs and significant donated and contributed resources. Tracy Robinson (and any other administrator who might be considering implementing an educational program using computers) would need to provide all these components to implement a similar program at her school, so she needs to include them all in her analysis of the program's cost.

This expanded notion of cost is discussed in the next section, which describes the procedures that were used to conduct the analysis.

COST ANALYSIS PROCEDURES

The Resource Approach to Cost

By the *cost* of an educational program we mean the value of all the resources that go into the program. According to this definition, one can determine the cost of a project by listing all the resources that were used and determining how much they are worth. Consequently, this approach is called the "resource approach" (Haggart, 1978) or the "ingredients approach" (Levin, 1983).

This analysis followed a similar procedure: We identified the resources used in the program, and we determined their value. In the next two sections these important procedures are discussed. Although this approach appears to be quite simple, it is not without pitfalls.

Identifying Resources. The first step, listing all of the ingredients or resources that were required to operate the program, appears to be quite easy. The list would surely include hardware, software, facilities, security, and teacher training.

The difficulty with this first step is that individual participants and observers are not usually aware of all the resources that support an activity. They tend to focus on the larger elements and ignore components that relate to the program only indirectly. These "background" resources include existing facilities, staff time that does not appear as a specific line item in a budget, and expenditures that are incurred by other agencies. Consequently, extra care was required in determining the ingredients that went into this project.

We were particularly lucky in this regard because the participating schools did not have to pay for the computers or the software (usually the two greatest cost items in a computer-based education program). As a result, the participants were more alert to small items and minor resources that were used in the project. In addition, because 89 schools were implementing similar programs, we had multiple observers to ensure that a thorough and reliable compilation of resources was obtained.

Determining Values. The second step in cost analysis is to determine the value of each ingredient. A dollar cost is usually calculated for each of the resources, because dollars offer a common metric for value that can be combined and compared. For example, a school might spend $3,375 to buy 15 computer desks to support the IBM Personal Computers.

Unfortunately not all resources have price tags to indicate their dollar value. For example, what was the value of the 6 hours of time that the two computer teachers donated on Saturday to assemble the 15 desks? Or the value of the chairs that were borrowed from other locations to go with the desks? These resources are necessary for the program to succeed, so it would be shortsighted to ignore them in analyzing the cost of the program, but they do not have an obvious market value like a product that is regularly bought or sold. What is their value?

An economist might answer this question by refering to the "opportunity cost" of the resource (Levin, 1975). This is the greatest value the resource would have in any foreseeable alternative use. According to this formulation, the value of a resource is the value of the opportunities that are foregone to use it for the given purpose (i.e., the value of the next most attractive alternative use). Unfortunately, the opportunity cost, although meaningful for many purposes, is not a practical measure of what a particular school will have to devote to acquire the given resource. For this reason it may not be the best measure for our purposes.

There are other problems that arise when one attempts to assign dollar values to resources that we need not discuss here. Some have precise solutions; others do not. Because the goal of this analysis was to provide practical information for school administrators, we modified the standard cost-analysis approach to avoid some of these difficult problems although still maintaining the accuracy of the resource description.

Cost/Resource Analysis: A Modified Approach

The approach used in this analysis sidesteps many of the difficult problems of cost analysis by using more than one scale of measurement. Rather than assigning dollar values to all the resources, we are content to use money as the measure in those cases where the resources were frequently purchased or exchanged, such as software. We use other natural scales for resources that are less meaningfully assessed in dollar terms, such as contributed staff time, and classroom space. In these cases the resources are compiled in their natural units—person hours, square feet, etc. Thus, the approach might be called a "cost/resource" analysis. For simplicity's sake, this chapter continues to use the term *cost,* but it means *cost/resource.*

In the present case this compromise seems justified. Each school presents a unique combination of staff expertise, existing facilities, community support, and so on. Consequently, it is more valuable for an administrator to know the resources required for a computer-education program in administratively meaningful units than it is to provide a single total annualized dollar cost. Decision makers can review these data in light of local conditions to assess their own costs/resource needs.

DISTRIBUTION OF COSTS/RESOURCES IN IBM PROGRAM SCHOOLS

A comprehensive list of the ingredients that went into the project is presented in Table 6.1. In the paragraphs that follow, each of these categories of ingredients is described, and the average level of resource use is indicated.[1] We also indicate the range of costs/resources that were observed across the 89 schools in the project. Where appropriate, dollar values are used; other-

---

[1] The averages reported in the cost/resource section should be used with care because many of the distributions were positively skewed (i.e., a few schools had high costs, whereas most had little or none). For example, two thirds of the schools did not acquire any additional hardware; their costs were zero. Yet, the average cost for additional hardware was almost $1,000 because the schools that did purchase hardware or peripheral devices spent large sums of money. The distributions for additional hardware, additional software, supplemental staff, furniture, telephone, air conditioning, and travel were of this type—most schools had little or no expenses in each of the categories, but a few schools had larger costs.

On the other hand, the distributions of costs for furniture, remodeling, supplies, and funded staff inservice training were close to uniform. This suggests that these resources were required in most locations and could be acquired in small, incremental units. *Most importantly,* the overall distribution of total expenditures was quite uniform. Thus, the average figure that was reported for total expenditures was a good representation of a "typical" school, and not merely a compromise between extremes.

TABLE 6.1
Summary of Resource Categories

Hardware

    Microcomputers and Printers (donated)
    Telecommunications Equipment and Services (donated)
    Maintenance and Repair
    Additional Hardware

Software

    Software (donated)
    Additional Software

Facilities

    Classroom Space
    Furniture
    Remodeling
        Rewiring
        Security
        Air Conditioning
        Telephone

Professional Services (donated)

    Summer Computer Institute
    Network Support
    Consulting

School Personnel

    Teaching Staff
        Summer Staff Development
        On-site Inservice Training
        Planning and Coordination
        Informal Inservice
    Administrative Support
    Supplemental Staff
    Travel

Materials and Supplies

Other

    Hidden Resources

wise, resource levels are reported in their natural units. Distributions are summarized in Table 6.2.

Hardware

Donated Microcomputers: $52,000. Each school received 15 IBM Personal Computers with 128K memory, color monitors, and two single-sided disk drives. Three dot matrix printers were also provided for each school.

Donated Telecommunication Equipment and Services: $1,000. Each school received a 300 baud intelligent modem, communications software, and 25 hours of time on a national telecommunications network.

Maintenance and Repair: 0-$4,700 (Mean = $886). Schools were required to make provisions for maintenance of the equipment after the expiration of the manufacturer's 90-day warranty. Those who purchased maintenance contracts from IBM or other vendors spent approximately $4,000 for these contracts. Those who made no special provisions paid for repairs as they became necessary.

Very few repairs were required. The most frequent problem that did occur involved broken hinges on the doors of the disk drives. One or two schools had more serious breakdowns.

In addition, a few of the schools installed surge protectors to prevent possible damage due to electrical power surges.

Additional Hardware and Peripherals: 0-$12,000 (Mean = $940). A few schools purchased letter quality printers, upgraded to double-sided disk drives, or bought other peripheral equipment, such as hard disks or large screen monitors.

Software

Donated Software: $20,000. The initial software that was donated to each school was valued at approximately $9,000. In addition, the schools were allowed to select software of their own choosing from a master list supplied by IBM during the course of the year. In the winter each school selected approximately $4,000 worth of software and in the spring they chose an additional $7,000.

Additional Software: 0-$2,200 (Mean = $404). Some schools used their own funds to purchase additional software that was not available on the donation list. This option included alternate word processing systems, specialized tutorial packages in health, and so on. The program staff were able to arrange significant discounts from a number of publishers, so most of

TABLE 6.2
Summary of Cost/Resources

Item	Mean	Range
Hardware		
Microcomputers (donated)	$52,000	
Telecommunications (donated)	$1,000	
Maintenance and Repair	$886	0- $4,700
Additionnal Hardware & Peripherals	$940	0-$12,000
Software		
Software (donated)	$20,000	
Additional Software	$404	0- $2,200
Facilities		
Classroom Space	500 sqft	330-1,200 sqft
Furniture	$1,560	0- $8,000 (and/or 15-30 tables & chairs)
Total Remodeling	$4,017	0-$19,500
Rewiring	$555	0- $4,000
Security	$727	0- $4,500
Air Conditioning	$1,345	0-$10,000
Telephone	$31	0- $478
Professional Services (donated)		
Summer Computer Institute	**	200-300 hrs*
Network Support	**	10-30 hrs*
Consulting	**	0-20 hrs*
School Personnel		
Teaching Staff Total	$3,670	0-$15,000 +50-1,000 hrs*
Summer Staff Development	**	0- $5,000 +300-500 hrs
On-Site Inservice Training	**	0-$12,000 +50-500 hrs
Planning and Coordination	**	50-200 hrs*
Informal Inservice	**	50-100 hrs*
Administrative Support	**	25-400 hrs*

6. COMPUTER-BASED EDUCATION COSTS   95

TABLE 6.2 *(continued)*

Item	Mean	Range
Supplemental Staff	$1,457	0–$15,000
Travel	$81	0– $1,000
Materials and Supplies	$678	0– $3,000
Other		
Hidden Resources		10–50 hrs*

Note: * indicates an estimated figure. ** indicates that there was not enough information to estimate a value.

these purchases were made at wholesale prices. Costs would be higher if a school tried to purchase the same software today.

Facilities

*Classroom Space: 300 sq. ft. – 1,200 sq. ft.
(Mean = 500 sq. ft.)*

Schools were required to provide a single facility to accommodate all 15 microcomputers. The smaller laboratories that contained only 300–400 sq. ft. of space were cramped and were difficult to use with a full class of students. Standard classrooms of 500–600 sq. ft. were adequate. Larger facilities offered many advantages. They made it possible to conduct group lectures and to accommodate individual seat work in conjunction with the use of the computers.

Many schools also provided either a secure storage room or a cabinet for storage.

*Furniture: 0–$8,000; 15–30 tables and chairs
Mean = $1,560)*

Every school equipped the computer area with tables and chairs. Most drew from their existing stock of furniture, but some purchased new tables specifically designed for use with computers. A few schools upgraded existing light fixtures, installed carpeting in the laboratory, or purchased movable display carts for one or two computers. One or two schools removed chalkboards and installed dust-free, liquid-marker writing surfaces.

Total Remodeling: 0–$19,500 (Mean = $4,017)

There was more variation in remodeling costs than in any other expenditure because schools' existing physical plants differed so greatly. Rarely were schools equipped to accept the microcomputers without some modifications. Typically, schools had to convert existing classrooms by limiting access, providing security systems, modifying electrical wiring, boosting air conditioning or cooling facilities, or making other adjustments. In a few of the schools major construction was required to provide an appropriate space.

The remodeling category included a variety of different activities. Separate subtotals were gathered for some of the most common items: rewiring, air conditioning, security, and telephone installations.

Rewiring: 0–$4,000 (Mean = $555). Rewiring was required in almost every school. Most standard classrooms were not equipped with adequate electrical circuits or sufficient numbers of outlets to handle the power demands of a laboratory of IBM microcomputers. In fact, although the IBM PCs with color monitors require more power than many other microcomputers, the power demands of *any* group of 15 microcomputers in a single location are likely to exceed the electrical capacity of most standard classrooms.

Security: 0–$4,500 (Mean = $727). Schools were responsible for the security of the computer laboratory. Security precautions included window bars, reinforced doors, and new locks. Some schools installed silent alarm systems wired directly to the police department or to a private security firm. A few schools purchased metal frames or locking devices that could be used to secure the machines to the desks. These "lock-down" devices cost as much as $250 a unit.

In a few instances the building that housed the computers was already fully secure, so no additional costs were incurred.

Air Conditioning: 0–$10,000 (Mean = $1,345). Computers do not operate efficiently under conditions of extreme heat (nor do teachers and students). Thus, a few schools had to make special arrangements to control the temperature by installing air-conditioning equipment that ensured safe computer operation. One or two were able to solve the problem by locating their machines in the school's coolest rooms.

Telephone: 0–$478 (Mean = $31). This project included a telecommunications component, and schools were encouraged to have a telephone line installed in the computer laboratory.

Donated Professional Services

Summer Computer Institute: 300–500 person-hours (estimated). Two staff members from the local Teacher Training Institute conducted a four-week intensive computer institute for three to five teachers from each school during the summer preceding the start of the program. Each summer institute was roughly the equivalent of three 3-unit courses at a college or university.[2]

Network Support: 10–30 person-hours per school (estimated). The staff of the local TTI provided additional training and support to the project schools during the year. They conducted day-long workshops for the core teacher group from four to six times during the year. Each meeting lasted between 3 and 6 hours and included additional instruction, introduction to new material, and sharing of experiences.

Consulting: 0–20 person-hours per school (estimated). Both the ETS project staff and the trainers from the local TTI were available on an as-needed basis to help with problems, offer ideas and suggestions, and provide support to schools throughout the year. Both groups were available for consultation by telephone and electronic mail. In addition, the TTI staff visited many of the schools to observe activities, talk with teachers and students, review program plans, and offer suggestions and advice. Some schools made far greater use of these resources than the other schools did.

School Personnel

Teaching Staff: 0–$15,000 + 50–1,000 person-hours (estimated). Mean = $3,670 + 500 person-hours (estimated)

Hundreds of hours of teacher time were devoted to the project, primarily for inservice training activities and in program planning and coordination. Schools had different methods of compensating teachers for the time they devoted to computer-related activities. In many cases the core group of teachers received salaries during the summer computer institutes, and funds were used to provide release time for this group to attend network workshops during the school year. Similarly, some schools were able to release the rest of the teachers for on-site inservice sessions of one type or another during the year. On the other hand, many of the human resources that were devoted to the project did not appear as cost items on any balance sheet. Teachers, for example, devoted many of their free hours to project-related activities.

Four major categories of teacher activity existed: staff development during the summer, formal on-site inservice training activities during the year, planning and coordination, and informal inservice activities. Each of these activities are discussed and, if possible, resource subtotals are estimated.

---

[2]Similar training might cost as much as $1,000 per person. Moreover, it is doubtful that courses of equal quality could be found in most locales.

Summer Staff Development: 0–$5,000 + 300–500 person-hours. On the average, four teachers from each school attended a month-long computer institute during the summer. Most public schools/districts provided stipends for these teachers in accordance with their standard policies for compensation. Public school teachers received approximately $1,000 each. Private school teachers frequently donated their time.

On-Site Inservice Training: 0–$12,000 + 50–500 person-hours (estimated). Most schools provided some type of formal inservice training for teachers who were not able to attend the summer computer institutes. (Some also included the classroom aides and support staff in these computer training workshops.) A typical program involved 2 to 4 hours for the entire staff, with more extensive follow-up workshops for interested groups. Thus, 50 to 500 person-hours might have been involved. Sometimes substitute teachers were hired to release staff for these inservice activities, and occasionally staff were compensated directly for this time. Quite often computer-related inservice activities were considered to be part of the teacher's regular, out-of-class responsibilities, and no extra compensation was involved. Teachers donated many hours because of their interest in the topic.

Planning and Coordination: 50–200 person-hours (estimated). The schools coordinated the ongoing use of the computers, including planning inservice training activities, scheduling access to the laboratory, and coordinating software acquisition. A few schools were able to designate one person as computer coordinator, reducing this person's classroom responsibilities so he or she could coordinate the computer program. Most often, however, teachers and administrators simply found time to accomplish these planning and coordination tasks in addition to their other responsibilities.

Informal Inservice: 50–100 person-hours (estimated). Most of the teachers who used the computers also received informal assistance from colleagues and students. In addition, teachers who became interested in the computers devoted large quantities of their own time practicing on the machines and developing lessons. These activities occurred before and after school, during free periods, and at home.

Administrative Support—25–400 person-hours (estimated)

School administrators are responsible for supervising all school activities, so some administrative time was devoted to the computer program. Principals and vice principals usually had some involvement in decisions concerning remodeling, inservice training, implementation, finances, community involvement, and so forth.

Supplemental Staff: 0–$15,000 (Mean = $1,457)

A few schools hired laboratory aides or technicians to assist with the computer activities. These were usually part-time positions.

Travel: 0–$1,000 (Mean = $81)

A few of the schools provided transportation or reimbursed teachers for the travel costs they incurred during the summer computer institutes.

Materials and Supplies: 0–$3,000 (Mean = $678)

Schools were encouraged to subscribe to journals and periodicals and to buy selected books that focused on computers in education. In addition, some schools purchased textbooks for teaching computer literacy or programming in BASIC or Pascal. Some teachers purchased their own books and magazines to supplement what was available at school.

Most schools provided blank disks for backing up new software and for teachers' use. Some schools also supplied classroom disks for students. All schools provided paper and ribbons for the printers. In addition, some purchased special marking pens for the liquid marker surfaces, and so forth.

Hidden Resources: 10–50 person-hours (estimated)

The hardest costs to identify are those that support the computer program indirectly as part of the general operation of the school or district. Specialized administrative support, such as accounting and financial services, was usually provided by the district office. Schools bore added utility costs and maintenance charges related to the microcomputers and the laboratory. Some small proportion of the total school and district resources in these areas are necessary to support the computer-education program.

AGGREGATED COSTS

It is informative to examine the total cost of the first year of the computer-based education project. To do this, costs have been aggregated into five logical categories: donated equipment, donated professional services, facilities, school human resources (not specifically supported by budget items), and school expenditures. The results are presented in Table 6.3.

To summarize the information in Table 6.3, the average school in this project spent roughly $15,000 during the first year of the program in supplementing the IBM donation (valued at $75,000).

TABLE 6.3
Aggregated Cost Summary

Category	Cost/Resource Level
Microcomputers and software (donated)	$75,000
Staff development and professional support (donated)	200–400 person hours
Classroom facilities	300–1200 sq. ft. & 15–30 tables and chairs
School/district expenditures	$460–$32,000 Mean = $15,200
Staff human resources (estimated)	50–2,000 person hours

TABLE 6.4
Initial Budget Considerations

Hardware	
Maintenance	$5,000–6,000
Large Screen Monitor(s)	1,000
Other Peripherals	5,000
Additional Software	5,000
Expendable Materials	
Diskettes for Backup	300
Diskettes for Students ($4 each student)	Variable
Printer Paper	500
Printer Ribbons	300
Curriculum Materials	
(typical per student expenditure)	Variable
Staff Training	
Travel to TTIs	Variable
Visiting Other Schools	Variable
Attending Conferences, Workshops, and Seminars	Variable

The school also provided all necessary facilities and hundreds of hours of school staff time. Finally, 200-300 hours of professional training and consultation were used.

COMPARISON WITH PRELIMINARY COST PROJECTIONS

It is interesting to compare the cost resource data with the estimated budgets that were provided to schools by ETS before the program began. A table describing budget considerations was distributed to participants before the program started to alert them to costs they were likely to incur as part of the program. This information is reproduced in Table 6.4.

ETS estimated that schools would need to budget approximately $17,000 (added to whatever amount was required to cover staff training) for participation in the project. As is seen, the total cost projected in Table 6.1 was remarkably close to the actual expenditures of the typical school in this project.

However, the distribution of costs was quite different from what was projected. The three largest cost items in Table 6.4 — maintenance, peripherals, and software — accounted for a very small part of the actual cost of the project in most schools. Despite their agreements, most schools did not buy maintenance contracts; almost none made capital outlays for additional peripheral equipment or for substantial software beyond that provided by the project. Instead, site preparation and staff training were the most costly items for the bulk of the schools.

DISCUSSION

A recapitulation of cost figures might be a bit overwhelming, because broad implications can be obscured by too many details. Consequently, we want to discuss only a few general points. First, we summarize the findings in broad terms. Second, we describe a number of relationships that emerged between costs and program characteristics. Third, a list of funding sources used by participating schools is shared. Finally, we entertain an important question that was not addressed in this study — did the benefits of the program justify the costs?

The Resources Needed for Computer-Based Education

When thinking about the cost of computer-based education, people tend to focus on the hardware and ignore the other resources that are necessary for program operation. This analysis helped to point out the significance of the nonhardware cost of operating a computer-based program.

The greatest nonhardware cost was *software*. In this project the value of the donated software was about 40% of the total value of the hardware. This percentage represents a major commitment of resources that many overlook when planning for educational computing. Of course, software needs are related to program goals (This relationship is discussed in the next section); nevertheless, it is important to recognize the potentially great cost of software.

The important nonhardware resource demands did not end with software. The typical school in this project spent an additional $15,000 on facilities and training, and it devoted hundreds of hours of staff time to inservice education and program implementation. In fact, supplemental expenditures ran as high as $30,000, a sum that represents about 60% of the cost of the hardware. Moreover, hundreds of hours of staff time were required to prepare and implement the project. This activity represents a significant refocussing of staff attention. It is a potentially dangerous error to dismiss nonhardware and software costs as "supplemental," as many people do. These data indicate that the supplemental resource demands of computer-based education are far from trivial.

The greatest single expenditure for schools in this project was for *remodeling,* (including rewiring, construction, security systems, and air conditioning). Although one or two computers may be absorbed into a classroom without special arrangements, expensive changes may be required to accommodate larger numbers of machines. Such costs are likely to be necessary in any extensive computer-based program, whether or not it follows the model incorporated into this program.

The second largest school expenditure was for staff *inservice training*. The cost of salaries and release time averaged more than $3,000 and was as high as $15,000. Moreover, these dollar figures reflected only a small part of the actual time spent by teachers and none of the professional assistance provided by ETS and TTI project staff. Staff development may well be the most significant, but most often overlooked, cost of computer-based education.

Finally, we should note that there was great variation in costs among the schools in this project. Despite common program goals and training, each school had different needs and capabilities, facilities and funding. Thus, there were significant differences in expenditures and human resources from one site to the next.

The Relationship Between Cost and Program Characteristics

The preceding discussion alluded to ways in which cost was affected by the program model adopted by ETS. Site visits and interviews with participants suggested several relationships between cost and program characteristics that appear to generalize beyond this one program to other computer-based education projects. The cost implications of four specific program elements are discussed in the following paragraphs: type of computer use, the extent of computer use in different subjects, the location of the computers, and the brand of microcomputer used.

However, before presenting these findings, it is important to caution the reader against basing program decisions primarily on cost considerations. Other factors must be considered as well. In fact, the most important factor is probably not cost, but effectiveness: Which program option will bring about the greatest educational benefits? Our own bias in this direction should be clear from the preceding five chapters. ETS required that the computers be placed in a single location rather than distributed across many classrooms because we believed this would increase their educational impact. We still advocate this arrangement despite its being somewhat more costly than other alternatives.

We offer the following cost data to help administrators make decisions, knowing that cost is just one factor that must be considered, along with considerations of effectiveness, availability, teacher preparation, community support, and many others.

The Effect of Type of Computer Use on Program Cost. Using the computer as a general purpose tool appears to be more costly than some other approaches to computer use, that is, using computers to teach programming. This is true primarily because of the added *training* cost associated with the tool orientation. There are also additional costs associated with software and supplies.

To understand these differences one must realize that computers can be used in many different ways. Among the most common uses of computers in education are computer-assisted instruction (CAI), using the computer as a general productivity tool (such as word processing, data base management systems, etc.), and computer programming. It takes less time to learn to use microcomputers for CAI than for word processing, data management, and other general tool applications. Similarly, the tool applications are more easily learned than programming. In this way, the program's orientation toward computer use will directly affect the amount of staff training that is required, and a program that involves more training will be more costly.

Software cost is also related to the way the computer is used. As before, an emphasis on the computer as a tool is a costly option, compared to some other orientations. To use the computer as a tool one must purchase software for word processing, for database management, for spreadsheets, for communications, for graphing, and the like. Each application requires a new piece of software (or one may buy a more expensive integrated package that includes two or three applications). In addition, software licensing agreements usually require that multiple copies of each type of software be purchased, so many machines can use the same package simultaneously. (It is worth noting that the current trend seems to be moving toward the sale of "school packages" of software at somewhat reduced costs.)

Programming, in contrast, requires very little software. Almost all microcomputers have a BASIC interpreter included as part of the system, and BASIC is the most popular programming language in schools. Some schools may purchase another language — Pascal, for example — but few elementary or secondary schools will maintain large libraries of programming languages.

Focusing on CAI will also require a large amount of software. Each disk contains a single lesson or cluster of related lessons. As a result, a large number of disks are required to cover a typical subject. Depending on how the program is implemented it might be necessary to have a separate copy of each disk for each microcomputer. Thus CAI is potentially the most expensive of the three approaches in terms of software. However, few schools are actually implementing CAI programs that cover the entire curriculum and incur such large resource commitments.

Finally, the orientation toward use of the computers — as a productivity tool, for CAI, or for programming — will affect the level of resources that are needed for supplies. In particular, word-processing applications generate more printed output than most other uses. Thus they require more paper and printer ribbons than other uses. Of course, supply costs are small in comparison with training and software costs.

The Effect of Extent of Use on Program Cost. Another important variable that affects the cost of computer-based education is the extent to which teachers throughout the school are involved in computer-related activities. Resource demands will be lower if fewer teachers are involved (and if previously trained teachers are responsible for most activities). The reason, once again, is the high cost of staff development.

Typically, schools that focus on programming rely on a very small number of teachers to do all the instruction. Even schools that emphasize CAI may structure computer use in such a way that only a few teachers interact directly with the computers. Involving few users requires less training and hence lowers the cost of the program.

This project emphasized computer use across all subject fields. Thus, it involved staff from many departments, including areas that are not usually concerned with technology, like English and foreign languages. This emphasis on widespread use meant that many more teachers were involved, including those who had little previous experience with computers. Consequently, more resources had to be devoted to inservice training.

The Effect of Location on Program Cost. The third relationship that was suggested by our experience with this project involves placement of the computers—either distributed throughout the school or centralized in a single location. More resources were used to accommodate the laboratory model than would have been required if the machines were distributed across many classrooms. The major factors in this relationship were the cost of remodeling, staffing, and security.

The typical school spent approximately $15,000 on remodeling (includng structural changes, rewiring, and air conditioning) and security devices to accommodate the microcomputer laboratory. Those few schools that could find funds also spent $5,000 to $10,000 for supplemental staff to monitor, assist in, and/or supervise the laboratory. (Though very few schools were able to hire supplemental staff in the first year, many expressed the desire to do such hiring in the future.)

Many of these costs would not have occurred had the machines been distributed in smaller numbers throughout the school. For example, additional wiring would not have been required in most schools if each computer had been assigned to a different classroom. Similarly, it is doubtful that major structural changes would have been made or that air conditioning would have been installed if the microcomputers had not been located in a single place.

Security costs would not have been eliminated, but we can speculate that they might have been reduced if the machines were distributed rather then centralized. This may seem counter-intuitive, because it is *easier* to protect the microcomputers if they are all located in one place. The facility itself can be secured (with locks, window bars, sonic alarms, etc.) rather than the individual computers. Obviously, it would be more expensive to secure multiple classrooms at this same level of protection.

On the other hand, if the computers had been distributed throughout the school, less elaborate precautions would probably have been taken. The laboratory itself became the focus of great pride, and schools did their best to make it a model facility. Thus they tended to procure the latest security systems. Spreading out the computers might have diffused attention to some degree, and authorities might have been satisfied with a lower level of security. To be sure, these observations are only speculation.

Overall, however, it does appear to be more costly to establish laboratories or centers than to distribute computers around the school.

The Effect of Brand of Microcomputer on Program Cost. The final resource-sensitive variable that emerged from this analysis was the brand of microcomputer. Some microcomputers cost more than others. Moreover, the price of related equipment and services varies depending on the brand of computer used. For example, maintenance costs differ from one brand to the next. As a general rule, the annual maintenance cost is typically 10% to 12% of a computer's list price. In this case, the IBM PCs were more expensive than many of the other brands of computers that are often used in schools, and their maintenance costs were higher as well. (We should note that microcomputer costs have dropped dramatically since the inception of this project. In particular, comparably equipped IBM PCs sell for about half the cost of the PCs used in this project.)

One must add, also, that a computer with a color monitor uses almost twice as much electrical power as a machine with a monochrome display. Power demands directly affect rewiring costs and utility bills. Moreover, different computers have different-sized consoles, and the size of the machine affects the choice of furniture. Some schools in the project purchased new tables or special desks to hold the computers. Other brands of computers might fit easily on existing furniture. Finally, software costs tend to be higher for some computers than for others. The same software, if it is available, will cost more on some brands than on others.

To summarize, we found that many features of the program model affected the level of resources that were needed. Focusing on general tool applications appears to be more expensive than either a CAI or programming orientation because of additional training costs, software requirements, and supplies. Similarly, an emphasis on broad use in many subject areas is more expensive than a narrower focus involving fewer teachers. Establishing a laboratory appears to require more resources than a distributed program. Finally, though absolute prices are changing rapidly, it is still true that some brands of computers will be more costly to obtain than others and will be more costly to maintain and support.

This section ends with the same caveat with which it began. It is important to keep in mind that cost should *not* be the only basis (or even the major basis) for program decisions. For example, there are many good reasons for preferring computing laboratories to distributed arrangements. Schools with computers in laboratory settings report greater numbers of teachers using the equipment, greater total number of hours of use, broader applications, and greater amount of time per user than schools with computers in other configurations (Center for the Social Organization of Schools, 1983b). The program developer should be aware of the cost implications of different choices but should not let cost unduly influence program decisions.

SOURCES OF FUNDS FOR COMPUTER-BASED EDUCATION

Where did the schools in the program find the funds that were used for example, in remodeling, supplemental equipment, and training? They used funds from four main sources: special state funds, district resources, private contributions, and local fund-raising activities. The mix of funding sources varied considerably from school to school, and there was no typical pattern of funding. In the following paragraphs we describe some of the fund-raising strategies that others may wish to emulate to finance computer-based education.

One place to look for funds to support computer-based education is special state programs. Some of the public schools in California qualified for state inservice education monies under a special funding provision enacted in Assembly Bill 551. The schools that had submitted plans and were awarded funding under AB551 were able to use the funds to cover the cost of schoolwide teacher training. For example, the money could be used to pay for substitutes and to fund "pupil-free" days at the beginning of the year, days that were devoted, in part, to computer training.

Many schools that participated in this project relied on their district to defray a large percentage of the cost. Specifically, most of the public schools did not have to concern themselves with the costs of site preparation, maintenance, and the like. The enticement of participating in the program and receiving a donation valued at about $75,000 was sufficient for the school districts to agree to provide adequate facilities and defray the cost of training the core group of teachers (when this was required by custom or contract).

Many schools in the project received private donations to help supplement the IBM gift. Private schools, in particular, relied on local donations to cover many of the costs that public school districts absorbed for their schools— remodeling and maintenance, for example. In these instances, individual donors often provided substantial contributions of goods and services. For example, a parent donated the air conditioning system at one school. In addition to single contributions, local parent booster groups became strong supporters of the new computer activities. They raised funds, donated equipment and services, and even helped to develop customized instructional software. In one school a booster group existed for each department and offered support and assistance to meet departmental needs.

Finally, a few of the schools were able to obtain donations of supplies and materials from local corporations. For example, one school received 1,000 blank disks from a local disk manufacturer.

One point worth noting is that corporate and institutional donors look favorably upon institutions that pledge some of their own resources to complement a gift. In fact, such demonstrations of local commitment are often required by a private donor. As it turns out, it is probably much easier to obtain local support (from the district administration, as well as parents and friends) if it is linked to an attractive donation than if it represents the entire cost of the project.

Many student organizations held fund-raising drives, such as candy sales and car washes, to raise funds to support the computer activities. The sale of blank disks for student use was a common fund-raising strategy. Schools found that they could buy computer disks very cheaply in large quantities, resell them to students (at a cost comparable to retail), and thus make a small profit to support the purchase of new software.

Finally, many schools raised money from adult education classes in computer literacy offered at night or on weekends for community members. In most districts, the fees from these classes could be used to support the computer program. In a few instances school staff donated their time as instructors; in others the tuition charges raised enough money to pay the teachers a salary and still return a small profit for the school. Demand for such classes seemed to be very strong in most of the schools where they were offered. Some of the teachers were even hired by their districts to teach supplemental classes for district staff from other schools.

As may be seen, schools raised funds to support computer education in several ways. Perhaps the most satisfying ways, and the most transportable, were those that focused on the computers themselves and people's natural interest in learning more about microcomputers.

A FINAL NOTE: IS COMPUTER EDUCATION WORTH THE COST?

After reviewing these data on the cost of computer education, a concerned educator might ask, "Were the benefits worth the cost?" This is a very important question. Though beyond the scope of the present analysis, other analytic approaches exist that can be used to examine this issue. Both cost-benefit analysis and cost-effectiveness analysis provide methods for comparing costs and benefits (Levin, 1983). The two techniques are similar to the methods employed here and also involve procedures for placing values on *outcomes* (such as achievement, grades, and motivation) much as we placed values on program ingredients.

There have been a number of cost-benefit analyses of the use of computers in education. Some concluded, favorably, that a computer-based instructional program did provide reasonable benefits at a feasible level of costs (Jamison, Suppes, & Butler, 1970; Ragosta, Holland, & Jamison, 1982). However, most of these analyses focused on the use of computers to deliver instruction. Their conclusions were based on the assumption that instruction by computer would replace existing teachers (Shavelson & Winkler, 1982). As a result, these studies cannot be readily generalized to a program such as the present one, which focused on the computer as a general-purpose tool.

In fact, the current widespread interest in educational computing is *not* based primarily on a wish to make it a surrogate teacher. Educators recognize that the computer is becoming an important element of our social and economic lives. As a result, many schools believe that it is their responsibility to familiarize students with the use and social implications of computers. In addition to computer-based instruction (the computer as tutor), this also includes teaching about the role of computers in society, computer programming, and the use of the computer as a general purpose tool for applications like word processing and database management. To our knowledge, these aspects of computer use have not been included in any of the cost-benefit analyses conducted to date. Thus, there is little evidence that can be used in answering the question of whether this effort was worth the cost.

Is computer-based education worth the cost? We do not know. Advocates argue that it is critical to introduce computers into the schools "at any cost." Critics suggest that the whole movement is another educational fad, of little lasting impact. Though we tend toward optimism on the subject, we cannot predict with certainty the future of educational computing. Nevertheless, school administrators feel growing public pressure to initiate computer-based programs, and there is rapid movement in this direction. We hope the data provided by this analysis helps administrators make more informed decisions about educational computing.

SUMMARY

The IBM project was conceived as a model for effective incorporation of computers in secondary education. IBM provided four components—hardware, software, training, and network support—while the schools provided facilities, staff, and other supplemental resources. The value of the computers and software was known in advance, but we could only speculate on the costs schools would incur by participating. Consequently, a cost analysis was undertaken to determine the actual level of resources used in the project.

This analysis showed that the schools' contributions were substantial. On the average, each school spent an additional $15,000 to prepare facilities, release staff for training, and provide supplemental equipment and software. In addition, the schools provided classroom space, furniture, maintenance, heating and electricity to support the computer laboratory. Furthermore, there was a major contribution of human resources; teachers and administrators spent hundreds of hours of their own time preparing to use the computer with students. The study also found that program costs were related to the manner in which the computers were used and the decision to locate them in a single laboratory facility. Finally, we identified a number of sources that can be used to provide funds to support computer education activities.

7 Program Impact

Randy Elliot Bennett
Susan Wilson

It is natural for community members, educators, policy-makers, and other interested persons to inquire about the worth of any innovative educational program. Such questions arise out of concern for whether the innovative program should be continued or, if the program is not already underway, whether similar efforts should be initiated. In considering the IBM program, these questions are of consequence. Clearly, the worth of the IBM program has implications for a variety of constituencies. At the school level, administrators participating in the original effort must decide whether to continue supporting the program beyond the start-up period. Similarly, those in other schools wanting to develop computer-education curricula must consider whether to implement a similar program. At the state and federal levels, policymakers must decide whether aspects of the IBM model are worth incorporating into their plans for computer education.

The worth of the IBM Secondary School Computer Education Program can be expressed in various ways. In the previous chapter, worth was examined with reference to the dollars and other resources invested in the program. In this chapter, we take a different perspective and examine program worth not through costs but through the impact or effects engendered by the program. We discuss these effects in terms of the attainment of program goals, the occurrence of unintended consequences, and the reactions of program consumers (Bennett, 1984, in press).

GOAL ATTAINMENT

Goal-attainment approaches measure program worth according to the extent to which the objectives of a program are achieved (Bloom, Hastings, &

Madaus, 1971). The approaches assume that goals were thoroughly reviewed at the beginning of the program to ensure their educational pertinence and value.

As stated in chapter 1, the purpose of the IBM program was to design and refine a model for promoting the effective use of microcomputers in secondary schools. In keeping with this purpose we specified as our goals the following:

1. To select a group of schools with diverse characteristics.
2. To increase student access to microcomputer hardware and software within these schools.
3. To increase the use of computers across a variety of subject areas, especially those in which computers have not been traditionally used.
4. To increase the number of teachers trained to use computers in education.
5. To increase the number of support relationships between secondary schools and local teacher-training and other educational institutions.

The rationale for and achievement of the first goal—to select a group of schools with diverse characteristics—was discussed in chapter 2. Data on the extent to which the remaining goals were achieved were gathered by ETS staff members from two sources. The first source was a questionnaire completed by ETS staff members in conjunction with school officials during site visits. The second source was a set of questions about school computer-education programs before and after the advent of the IBM program. This set of questions was contained in a mail survey responded to by personnel in 72 schools.[1] Together, these data sources offer information on the extent to which the goals of the IBM program were achieved.

---

[1]Eighty-eight responses were received for the preprogram questionnaire and 72 for the postprogram questionnaire. Analyses were conducted only on the 72 schools submitting both preprogram and postprogram data. This group constitutes 81% of the total number of schools participating in the IBM Program. The group of 16 schools omitted from the analysis is similar in its responses to the group of 72 schools on most items contained on the preprogram questionnaire including minority, female, and total enrollment, mean class size, and percentage of students enrolled in different curricula. Some differences in preprogram responses, however, were noted. Students in omitted schools were somewhat less likely to learn to use or program computers in computer education courses and computer programming courses, but more likely to use the machines to learn subject-matter content. Fewer students in the omitted schools were taught BASIC, though more students participated in supervised computer clubs. Machines in these schools were available to students outside of scheduled classes more hours per day. Finally, omitted schools were less likely to have received computer support or training services from a college or university.

Increasing Access to Microcomputer Hardware and Software

The effective use of computers in education requires that students have adequate access to microcomputer hardware and software. Without such access, opportunities for learning to use computers as supplements or for learning about computers are clearly limited. To address the question of hardware and software access, we present evidence regarding changes in the number of computers and software packages, the location of computers, and student use of the machines.

Changes in the Number of Computers and Software Packages. The most direct way of increasing student access to microcomputers is to raise the number of machines available for student use. The IBM program addressed this need by donating 15 personal computers to each participating school. Data gathered from 31 site-visit questionnaires indicate an increase of 16 machines per school (preprogram median = 13; postprogram median = 29), suggesting that the IBM donation was the primary source of additional school hardware resources attained during the program period.

In conjunction with increasing the number of machines available for student use, the IBM program also attempted to increase the number of different software packages in schools. From the site-visit responses for 28 schools, the median number of different packages available before the program was 4, while 23 were reported to be in-house after the program donation. The responses to mail questionnaires produced similar results: a median of 6 packages prior to the program and 25 after. Both data sources indicate an increase of 19 different software packages, an increase again almost exclusively owed to the IBM donation.

Changes in the Locations of Computers. The location of computers in a school can serve to limit or facilitate student access (Center for the Social Organization of Schools, 1984a). For example, the location of computers in specific subject-matter classrooms limits access to only students enrolled in those classes. In contrast, placement in a centralized lab has been found to be associated with student use for more hours per week, longer turns at the computer per student, and regular use by a larger number of teachers (Center for the Social Organization of Schools, 1984a). To maximize access, ETS and IBM, therefore, recommended that computers be placed in labs that could be used by several different classes as well as by individual students on an ad hoc basis.

Table 7.1 depicts the change in the location of computers used by students before and after the advent of the IBM program. As the table shows, the

TABLE 7.1
Change in Percentage of Schools Placing Computers in Various Locations ($n = 72$)

Location	Percent Before Program	Percent After Program	Change in Percentage Points
Computer Lab	69	90	21
Library/media center	19	39	20
Department Office	17	26	9
Classroom	67	67	0
Other	13	10	−3

largest increases are found for those locations that grant the greatest access: the computer lab and the library media center.

Changes in Student Computer Use. Although increases in hardware and software and changes in the location of computers suggest greater student access, the extent of change in actual student use provides stronger evidence that increased access actually occurred. Prior to the IBM program, the median percentage of students in a school using computers on a daily basis was 8%. After the advent of the program, this proportion rose to 18%. Interestingly, the median amount of time per day that an average student spent using computers for instructional applications increased only slightly from 37.5 to 40 minutes. Coupled with the rise in the proportion of students using computers, this result suggests that computing resources were used more to grant access to a greater number of students than to increase the amount of computing time given a limited group.

Also relevant to student use are data on extra-curricular activities. Prior to the program, the median number of students regularly participating in supervised computer clubs was zero; after the program, this figure rose to 10. Likewise, the median amount of time per school day in which computers were regularly available for student use outside of scheduled class activities doubled from 1 to 2 hours.

In sum, the amount of hardware and software, the placement of computers in accessible locations, the percentage of students using computers, and the amount of time computers were available all increased concurrently with the IBM program. These increases provide strong support for the contention that student access to computers was increased in the sampled schools. Finally, that no significant increases in hardware and software were apparent outside of the IBM donation suggests that the observed changes in student access were due to the IBM program and not to other, unrelated sources.

Increasing the Use of Computers Across Subjects

The IBM program was designed also to encourage use of computers across a wide range of school subjects. Underlying this goal was a desire to bring computing to greater numbers of students and, particularly, to students traditionally excluded from computing activities (e.g., those not enrolled in advanced mathematics or computer programming courses). Because computer programming has little direct practical application in many secondary-school courses (e.g., in the arts and humanities), we chose to deemphasize it. Instead, we focused on the use of generic applications programs—that is, word processors, database managers, graphics and graphing tools, and spreadsheets—as supplements to traditional learning activities.

To what extent were computers actually used for programming and nonprogramming purposes across subject areas? Table 7.2 shows the change in use of computers for *nonprogramming* purposes in courses before and after the IBM program. By far, the largest single increase, 57 percentage points, is associated with English, patently a course in which computers have not been traditionally used. The large increase here is most probably due to the use of word processing, a natural aid in writing essays, compositions, reports, short stories, and other activities typically assigned in this high-school subject.

The remaining 11 subjects experiencing increases greater than or equal to 15 percentage points represent a variety of secondary-school curriculum areas. Particularly noteworthy, however, is the strong representation of those areas not traditionally tied to computing: the social sciences (economics and social studies), fine arts (music and art), and courses for special populations (independent study, special education, and programs for gifted students). Only three subjects—science, business education, and mathematics—are commonly associated with computing.

Table 7.3 shows the change in student programming activity for different courses before and after the IBM program. The data contained in the table are striking: only one increase, for advanced computer programming courses, is greater than 15 percentage points. The magnitude of this increase is moderate when compared with those found for the nonprogramming use of computers in high school courses; it suggests that, relative to programming, substantial progress was made in incorporating computers in the nontraditional subject areas.

Although progress was made in using computers in many curricular areas, it is nevertheless true that programming was the most popular use, particularly programming in BASIC. For example, the median number of students per school who were taught BASIC before the IBM program was 70; after the program was initiated, the figure nearly doubled to 130.

Table 7.4 presents the different ways in which teachers used or taught about computers during the IBM program. As the table demonstrates, 96%

TABLE 7.2
Change in Percentage of Schools Indicating Courses in which Computers were used for Nonprogramming Purposes ($n = 72$)

Course	Percent Before Program	Percent After Program	Change in Percentage Points
English	13	70	57
Science	18	58	40
Social Studies	7	39	32
Business Ed	50	79	29
Economics	3	29	26
Independent Study	13	38	25
Special Ed	21	44	23
Mathematics	49	71	22
Art	3	24	21
Foreign Language	6	26	20
Music	3	21	18
Programs for Gifted Students	6	21	15
Computer Ed	57	71	14
Advanced Computer Programming	26	39	13
Vocational Ed	18	30	12
Distributive Ed	3	10	7
Home Economics	3	8	5
Physical Ed	0	3	3
Health	0	3	3
Other	14	15	1
Computer Programming	61	56	−5

of the 72 schools responding stated that teachers used computers to teach programming. The next most popular use of computers was in teaching hardware and software procedures (93%). Following these two activities, however, are three that are not as clearly tied to programming: student problem solving (82%), instructional games (78%), and simulations (78%). The conclusion we draw is similar to the one derived from our site visits: on the whole, schools made substantial use of computers as both subject of and supplement to instruction.

In sum, schools in the IBM program mail survey sample increased their use of computers across a variety of subject areas, concurrent with the program.

TABLE 7.3
Change in Percentage of Schools Indicating Courses in which Computers were used for Programming Purposes ($n = 72$)

Course	Perdent Before Program	Percent After Program	Change in Percentage Points
Advanced Computer Programing	32	50	18
Independent Study	10	22	12
Mathematics	31	42	11
Programs for Gifted Students	6	13	7
Music	0	6	6
Business Ed	26	31	5
Special Ed	1	6	5
Art	0	4	4
English	3	7	4
Social Studies	0	3	3
Computer Programming	71	74	3
Science	8	10	2
Distributive Ed	1	3	2
Home Economics	0	1	1
Physical Ed	0	1	1
Health	0	0	0
Economics	1	1	0
Vocational Ed	7	7	0
Computer Ed	54	54	0
Foreign Language	1	1	0
Other	6	1	−5

We have little direct evidence to support the contention that this increase was actually caused by the program. However, it is unlikely that factors independent of the program could have acted upon such a geographically and socioeconomically diverse set of schools during the same period. Therefore, we conclude that the program was responsible for the observed change.

Increasing the Number of Trained Teachers

Although many different resources are important to the success of computer-education programs, one of the most critical is the teacher. Yet it is

TABLE 7.4
Percentage of Schools Indicating Ways in which Teachers Used or Taught About Computers (*n* = 72)

Activity	Percentage of Schools Indicating Computer Use
Teach programming	96
Teach hardware and software procedures	93
Student problem solving	82
Instructional games	78
Run simulations	78
Teach computer applications	76
Information retrieval	75
Materials generation (tests or worksheets)	74
Teach data processing	73
Drill in math, spelling, etc.	70
As a tutor (teach content)	68
Demonstrate concepts	68
Leisure time activity	67
As a calculator	64
Student analysis of data	60
Teach about the role and impact of computers in society	57
Teach terminal operation	57
Teach history of computers	56
Teach about computer careers	54
Instructional management	53
Other	15
Score tests	13

clear that relatively few secondary-school teachers possess the skills necessary to teach with or about computers. Moreover, those teachers that do develop such skills often move into administrative positions or to more lucrative jobs in industry (Shavelson, Winkler, Stasz, Feibel, Robyn, & Shaha, 1984). Because of these facts, the IBM program sought to increase the number of teachers trained to teach with or about computers.

Several pieces of data support attainment of this training goal. The most direct evidence of attainment is that the median number of teachers per school described as "highly qualified" to teach about computing rose from three on the preprogram questionnaire to five on the postprogram instrument. The magnitude of this change is slightly less than the three-to-five teachers per school trained through the TTIs. This result is understandable given that (1) many of the teachers who were sent for TTI training were relative novices and (2) "high qualifications" to teach about computing may take several years to develop.

In addition to changes in the number of teachers qualified to teach about computing, less direct evidence relevant to attainment of this goal is available. For example, the median number of staff members teaching courses that used or taught about computers rose from three to seven over the course of the program. At the same time, the median number of teachers owning their own microcomputers or terminals also rose from three to five. These results suggest that more teachers are gaining experience with computers by teaching courses that use them and by owning them.

On the whole, the data imply that the number of teachers trained to teach with or about computers increased coincidentally with the IBM program. The strong emphasis on developing qualified personnel provided through both the TTI summer sessions and local school inservice programs make it likely that the increase in trained teachers was in large part owed to the IBM effort.

Increasing the Number of Support Relationships

Because relatively few secondary-school educators are expert in the operation of computer-education programs, the development of a new program requires substantial support from sources external to the school. Such sources may include local colleges and universities, state education departments, schools already running successful programs, and other technical assistance agencies. The support these institutions provide may be informational or may simply take the form of encouragement during difficult times. Realizing the need for such support, the IBM program attempted to increase the number of support relationships between secondary schools and local teacher-training and other educational institutions.

The primary mechanism for fostering support relationships was the TTI. In 7 of the 12 cases, the TTI was a college or university. In two cases the TTI was associated with a state agency and in two a consortium of school districts. In the one remaining case, the TTI was located within a school district.

Table 7.5 presents data identifying the percentage of schools receiving support and training services from different sources before and after the IBM program. As the table shows, the largest increase is for service from colleges and universities. This result is not entirely surprising because the majority of TTIs were of this institutional type.

TABLE 7.5
Change in Percentage of Schools Using Different Sources of Support (n = 72)

Support Source	Percent Before	Percent After	Change in Percentage Points
College or university	26	50	24
Local industry	10	13	3
Computer consortia	13	14	1
Individual	13	13	0
State agency	19	18	−1
Computer store	28	19	−9

With respect to this final goal of the IBM program, moderate success was achieved. Support relationships with colleges and universities were increased, although no substantial effects were detected for consortia, state agencies, or local industry. The fact that most TTIs were postsecondary institutions and that support relationships were increased with this group and no other suggests that the IBM program played a causal role in fostering the development of these relationships.

Conclusion

The results from preprogram and postprogram mail surveys and from site-visit questionnaires support the contention that the major goals of the IBM program were achieved within the sampled schools. Further, the program appears to be the logical cause of these effects in most cases, though as in much social science research, definitive links are difficult or impossible to prove.

RELATED EFFECTS

The concept of related effects is most clearly illustrated with reference to the production of pharmaceutical medicines. Such medicines are typically intended to achieve a limited set of goals — the relief of angina through the use of nitroglycerin, or the elimination of infections through antibiotics. Unfortunately, medicines sometimes have unintended or, as we have termed them, related effects. Such effects range from relatively minor ones like headache and nausea to death.

Educational programs can also have related effects, that is, effects that are not reflected in a program's stated goals (Scriven, 1974). Such effects can be positive, as when overall student attendance is increased by a free hot-lunch program; or negative, as when the same program draws students to the cafeteria during class time. With regard to the IBM program, we discuss three types of related effects, specifically, on students, teachers and institutions. Data on these effects are derived from the schools' responses to the post-program questionnaire.

Effects on Students

Table 7.6 presents the responses of school staff to questions about the cognitive and social effects on students participating in the program. Under the rubric of cognitive effects, 71% of those responding said that "more" or "much more" academic learning by above-average students was taking place as a result of having more microcomputers; in contrast, 57% noted "more" or "much more" learning by average students, and 47% saw improvement in below-average students. This perceived effect for different levels of ability agrees with findings from the National Survey of School Uses of Microcomputers (Center for the Social Organization of Schools, 1983a). One possible explanation for the perceived effect on high-ability students is that these

TABLE 7.6
School Responses Regarding the Cognitive and Social Effects on Students of Having More Computers

	Percent Checking Each Option[a]			
Cognitive Variable	Much More	More	A Little More	No More
Academic learning by "above-average" students ($n = 69$)	29	42	13	13
Academic learning by "average" students ($n = 66$)	11	46	24	11
Academic learning by "below-average" students ($n = 68$)	15	32	33	14
Students doing work more appropriate to their own ability level ($n = 67$)	28	40	17	8
Social Variable				
General Enthusiasm for school by students using computers ($n = 70$)	63	29	6	0
Students taking the lead in helping other students with their questions ($n = 69$)	39	39	15	3
Students working successfully on their own without direct supervision from the teacher ($n = 70$)	51	36	10	0

[a]Total percentages for each question do not equal 100% because of missing responses.

students typically receive preferential access to microcomputers. Results from the National Survey suggest that such preferential access is typical within secondary schools (Center for the Social Organization of Schools, 1983c, 1984). For IBM program schools, however, the extent of access granted different ability groups is not known. We should note one more result: The bulk of respondents in the IBM program (68%) reported "more" or "much more" instances of students doing work appropriate to their own ability levels. This finding suggests benefits, regardless of cognitive capability, to all students working with computers.

Interesting results are also found for social effects. For example, 92% of those responding noted "more" or "much more" general enthusiasm for school by students using computers. Seventy-eight percent indicated "more" or "much more" instances of students taking the lead in helping their peers. Finally, 87% agreed that there were "more" or "much more" instances in which students worked successfully without direct supervision from the teacher. These results agree with those of the National Survey of School Uses of Microcomputers, which also found teachers perceiving substantial changes on these social-learning variables (Center for the Social Organization of Schools, 1983a).

One final set of social effects is relevant to our discussion. Many investigators have reported that females and minority students are often underrepresented in computer-education programs (Campbell & Gulardo, 1984; Lockheed & Frakt, 1984; Miura & Hess, 1983). Various hypotheses have been suggested for the phenomenon including less interest in computing among females, fear of what is perceived as a mathematically related activity, avoidance of a seemingly male-dominated domain, and the imposition of such barriers as prerequisite high-level math and science courses. Regardless of the cause, this type of differential access serves to widen racial and gender inequities by limiting the development of important academic and job-related skills within these groups.

The IBM program worked explicitly to foster equal access at the program level by establishing as a goal the inclusion of schools representing all the inherent diversity of American education. Evidence presented in chapter 2 does support the claim that equity had been achieved *across* schools (i.e., by creating an ethnically and socioeconomically diverse group); but it is reasonable to ask whether mechanisms may have operated to produce differential access *within* those schools once the machines had been placed there — outside the control of IBM and ETS.

Data on the composition of student groups using machines within program schools come from the site-visit questionnaires. Responses to these questionnaires ($n = 28$) indicate that the median percentages of students involved with computers were 49.5% for females and 50.5% for males. These figures are virtually indistinguishable from the equivalent proportions in the American secondary school population (U.S. Bureau of the Census, 1984). Figures for minority representation suggest a similar conclusion: The median percentages involved with computers were 15% for minority and 85% for majority groups ($n = 27$). With allowance for sampling error, the percentages are equivalent to those for the secondary school population.[2,3]

Effects on Teachers

Two findings from our school survey are pertinent to the effects on teachers of having more computers. First, 59% of respondents ($n = 68$) report "more" or "a little more" rapport between teachers and students. Increased rapport may be due to the situation (reportedly a frequent one) in which students know more about computing than the teacher does. In such a situation, the resourceful teacher has found ways to work collaboratively with students, both to learn from them and to gain their assistance as lab or course assistants.

A second interesting effect on teachers is the reported lack of disagreement over curriculum and expenditure issues. With any educational innovation, especially one that implies the establishment of a new curricular area, disagreement is to be expected. Disagreement might focus on such issues as course content or the grade levels at which different aspects of that content should be introduced, or which students should learn the content, or how much of the school budget should be invested in it. In our sample, however, 68% of respondents ($n = 67$) reported that there was "no more" (50%) or "a little more" (18%) disagreement among teachers, a finding that suggests either general agreement on these issues or, perhaps more likely, on issues that have not yet become vexing for most teachers.

Effects on Institutions

The related effects on institutions of the IBM program include those on computer program planning and coordination, and community involvement. Within the category of program planning and coordination, 44% of school officials stated that their school had had a computer coordinator or computer science department chairperson before the advent of the IBM program. After the program, the percentage of respondents reporting the presence of such a functionary nearly doubled to 83. This concurrent increase in

---

[2]For the 1982 school year, the percentages of males and females attending secondary school were 51 and 49, respectively. Approximately 82% of the school population was classified as white and 18% as minority (U.S. Bureau of the Census, 1984).

[3]Ninety-five percent confidence intervals for these percentages are 4% to 26% for the minority figure and 73% to 97% for the majority point estimate. The confidence intervals are wide because the point estimates are based on such small samples.

the number of positions is important; it suggests a growing acceptance within the schools of the legitimacy of computer-education activities and a concern for the continued planning and coordination of these programs.

The most important change in community involvement occurring during the IBM program was in adult education. Before the program, 49% of survey respondents stated that their school facilities were employed to teach adults to use or program computers. This percentage rose to 70 after the program, confirming the frequent presence of computer education for adults observed during site visits. This type of community interaction is critical, for it provides an opportunity for the school to demonstrate directly the value of its services to its financial backers.

Conclusion

Our data suggest the occurrence of several effects in the IBM Program school sample not included in the program goal statements. The data imply increased learning, positive changes in the social structure of the classroom, and equal access for female and minority students. In addition, more cooperation was noted between teachers and students, as well as increased coordination of computer education and growing community involvement. Finally, the possibility was raised of differential access based on ability level.

CONSUMER REACTION

Any useful assessment of program worth must take into account the personal reactions of those served by the program (Kiresuk, Lund, & Schultz, 1981). Such reactions provide evidence of the program's responsiveness to consumer needs, and in so doing speak to the program's "social" worth or validity (Wolf, 1978). In addition, the analysis of consumer reaction helps identify problem areas to be addressed in future efforts.

In this section, we examine the degree of satisfaction with the IBM program from the point of view of its consumers. We define consumers as those who were direct recipients of the program's services: TTI personnel, school personnel, and students.

Data on consumer satisfaction come from several sources tapped by ETS staff during the final phase of the program after its termination. The reactions of TTI representatives were gathered through the postprogram telephone interviews described in chapter 4. The opinions of principals and teachers were derived from site visits and from a series of meetings with school personnel held at the end of the program. Although students were important consumers of program services, no data were available to document directly their reactions to the program.

TTI Staff Reaction

Information from telephone interviews regarding the TTI representatives' assessment of the program focused on four issues: hardware configuration, software, training, and administrative factors.

Hardware. TTI representatives were generally satisfied with the donated hardware configuration. Such a reaction is understandable given the advanced capabilities of the donated hardware as compared with those of microcomputers typically found in secondary schools. Beyond general satisfaction with the hardware, two specific areas of dissatisfaction were noted. First, the majority of the staff indicated that machines were needed with more memory and with double-sided diskette drives. The donated configuration (128K memory and two single-sided disk drives) was adequate at the beginning of the program, but it became less so as software requiring greater capabilities was released.

TTI staff were also concerned with the number of donated printers (three per school). In their view, the lack of printers hindered the acquisition of computer skills in such areas as word processing, because time that students could have spent computing was instead spent waiting on line for a printer.

Software. Reaction to the software component of the program varied widely. Some TTI representatives thought the software excellent; others were extremely dissatisfied with the packages that were offered. The PFS series, The Instructor, Question, Multiplan and Delta Drawing were mentioned as good selections, whereas Easywriter was criticized as being difficult to learn. Once again, the trainers thought that many teachers did not perceive the applicability of the generic software to their courses and were, in addition, frustrated by the lack of appropriate educational software.

The method of choosing and distributing software was also a source of concern. The concept of a core software list followed by two optional lists was viewed positively, but the selection and distribution of software were perceived as needing improvement. Many of the representatives thought that the TTIs should have been more directly involved in selection and distribution. The lack of involvement was seen to cause confusion in ordering and consequent delays in delivery.

Training. The TTI representatives also offered their retrospective opinions of the training delivered at ETS in May 1983, and of the training provided to school staff members that summer. The ETS training was seen as an important factor in guaranteeing success of the program. Most of the TTI staff rated the training as "excellent" or "very good," and some said it was the best training that they had ever participated in. Several institutions later modeled their own summer training after the ETS session.

About half the TTI representatives viewed their own summer teacher training as highly successful; the remainder regarded their programs as adequate, but they were disappointed that the training did not go so well as anticipated. This latter group felt that many problems could have been resolved if there had been more time for preparation between the ETS training and their own sessions and for the teachers to learn the hardware and develop plans to integrate the software with the curriculum before the start of the school year.

Administrative Factors. Trainers expressed dissatisfaction with three administrative aspects of the program. First, dissatisfaction was expressed with the degree of support and commitment shown by some school administrators. More cooperation and involvement of the school principals and district administrators from the onset of the project would, according to TTI staff, have made the IBM program easier to implement.

Second, the level of financial support provided by some districts was a cause of concern. Funds were needed to support such necessities as teacher released time, substitutes, inservice training, telecommunications, and hardware maintenance. Those districts in which such funds were not allocated were viewed as having less effective programs.

Finally, the duration of the program was viewed as inadequate. A 1-year period made each component of the program too concentrated. Several representatives thought that a 3-year period was the minimum necessary to implement an effort of this magnitude.

School Staff Reactions

To get the reactions of school staff to the IBM program, ETS personnel held group meetings with principals and teachers in every network during March and April 1983. From these meetings, we were able to confirm earlier reports of satisfaction and dissatisfaction—as well as identify new sources of contentment and concern—with respect to three areas: hardware and software, training and network support, and administrative factors.

Hardware and Software. Comments made at the meetings about hardware and software generally agreed with our earlier perceptions. School personnel were particularly pleased with the overall quality and quantity of the hardware and with the notion of centralizing computers in a lab. In addition, some school staff applauded the program's choice of applications software. Areas of concern included selected aspects of the hardware configuration (i.e., memory, disk drives), and the process and content of software selection.

Training and Network Support. Most of the teachers had very positive reactions to training delivered by the TTIs. Several teachers indicated that the training had had an additional affective impact: It had given them the confidence needed to begin using the computers in the classroom. The lack of emphasis on ways to integrate the computer with the secondary-school curriculum was cited as the major shortcoming of summer training.

The participants also had generally positive reactions to the program's network support services. The monthly TTI meetings and other network activities were reported to be valuable by participants (as well as by the large majority of those polled during site visits). Staff members particularly appreciated the opportunity to meet and share ideas with other teachers and administrators.

Administrative Factors. Lack of administrative commitment was once again mentioned as the program element most in need of improvement. Like TTI staff, the teachers believed that greater commitment from school and district administrators was necessary to implement the computer education program successfully. As they saw it, one of the major weaknesses was that firmer commitments had not been obtained from administrators at the beginning of the program. The absence of administrative support resulted in the repeated frustration and dissatisfaction of high school staff throughout the year.

The idea that IBM involvement would end at the close of the 1983-1984 school year also concerned many persons, who felt the need for continued support during the coming year. In fact, the majority of participants in the meetings planned to continue some form of network contact, ranging from formal gatherings to telephone consultation.

Despite their concerns, most of the meeting participants were very positive about the overall effects of the program. Many acknowledged that the IBM program gave a huge boost to their districts' computer education efforts. Principals and teachers were particularly satisfied with the flexibility offered by the program's philosophy of using the computer as a tool. This flexibility allowed each school to adapt the program to its own curriculum and, in addition, fostered the use of the computer by students and teachers who might otherwise not have been involved in computer education.

Conclusion

Our analysis of TTI and school staff members' reactions to the IBM program suggests areas of both satisfaction and concern. Staff members were most satisfied with the hardware, training, and network support components of the program. In addition, teachers and principals were impressed with the project's positive impact on computer education in their schools. Concern was most commonly expressed with administrative aspects, particularly the level of support offered by some school administrators and the 1-year duration of the project. Finally, consumers disagreed over the software component, some finding the selection of programs adequate and others finding the choice too limited.

SUMMARY

This chapter has assessed the worth of the IBM program through an analysis of its impact. *Impact* was defined as the attainment of program goals, the occurrence of unintended effects, and the reactions of program consumers. In the schools studied, the IBM program was found to be associated with increases in: (a) student access to microcomputer hardware and software; (b) the use of computers across a variety of subject areas, especially those in which computers have not traditionally been used; (c) the number of teachers trained to use computers in education; and (d) the number of support relationships between secondary schools and local teacher training institutions.

The unintended effects associated with the IBM program were found to be generally positive. More learning, positive changes in the social structure of the classroom, and equal access for female and minority students were reported. More cooperation between teachers and students, as well as increased coordination of computer education and greater involvement of the school with the community were noted. The possibility of differential access based on student ability level was raised.

Finally, the reactions of program consumers were assessed. Consumers were generally satisfied with the hardware, training, and support components of the program and less content with the software, the school administrative support, and the duration of the donation effort.

8 Summary and Recommendations

Hugh F. Cline
Martin B. Schneiderman

In this chapter we review the characteristics of the IBM Secondary School Computer Education Program that made it a particularly significant educational innovation. Microcomputers may come to play an important role in reforming and strengthening the nation's secondary schools, and the IBM program can contribute substantially to that goal. The program embodied a major effort to explore strategies for using the microcomputer as a learning tool in a wide range of curricular and extracurricular activities and to develop a model for implementing such projects. For this reason, we believe it is valuable to document the program's most significant features for the consideration, adoption, and adaptation of educators.

We also present specific recommendations for schools developing their own computer education programs. These recommendations are organized around the themes of program design, hardware and software, professional development, support activities, and cost considerations.

SIGNIFICANCE OF THE PROGRAM

The IBM Program was a pioneering undertaking. It was the first large-scale partnership between the IBM Corporation and secondary schools that focused directly on using personal computers in many subject areas. Although many IBM branch offices, plants, and laboratories had previously donated hardware and services to neighboring schools, never before had the Corporation been involved in a large-scale secondary school donation program.

Other computer manufacturers had established school-donation programs, but none had attempted the scope or magnitude of the IBM Program.

Apple Computer's "Kids Can't Wait" program provided a single Apple IIe to every school that applied for one in California, where a tax incentive had been provided by the state legislature. Tandy Corporation offered every school teacher several hours of introductory computer instruction at one of their many retail computer centers.

No manufacturer, however, had designed and initiated as comprehensive a computer-education program as IBM, a program that incorporated hardware, software, training, and network support. As we have seen in chapter 7, the program was effective across a wide variety of secondary schools in: (a) increasing student access to hardware and software in various curriculum areas; (b) training many teachers to use computers in their classes; and (c) fostering positive change in the social structure of the classroom, including an increased enthusiasm for learning.

In addition to representing a unique $8 million corporate school collaboration, this program was a noteworthy educational innovation. There were several distinguishing features:

1. diversity among the participating schools
2. use of the computer as a tool
3. emphasis on female and minority participation
4. centralized computer laboratories
5. network structure
6. layered training program
7. telecommunications capability

Diversity was an important element because it increased the likelihood that the model could be generalized nationwide. As explained in chapter 2, we consider it important to include many different types of schools varying across several relevant dimensions, including social class, location, and affiliation (i.e., public, independent, or religious-affiliated). In addition, we selected schools serving special populations to further expand the variety of students included in the program.

Another important aspect of the program was its emphasis on using the microcomputer as a tool to facilitate learning in many different subjects. By encouraging the use of generic application packages for word processing, database management, electronic spreadsheets, and graphics production, rather than only programming languages, we promoted the use of microcomputers by larger numbers of students. As reported in chapter 7, the data collected from the participating schools showed substantive increases in nonprogramming computer use in English, social sciences, and fine arts.

To accomplish this goal, we specifically requested that principals select teachers from many different disciplines to attend the summer training. The data presented in chapter 4 clearly demonstrate that diversity of teacher's subject-area expertise was achieved. Finally, the software donated to the schools also included a wide variety of generic application packages that were adopted for nonprogramming uses of the PCs.

Equal access to the PCs was also an important program component. The National Survey of School Uses of Microcomputers, conducted by Johns Hopkins University, gives evidence that computer education to date has been largely confined to teaching a small number of advanced students to write programs (Center for the Social Organization of Schools, 1984a). In the typical U.S. high school, advanced mathematics courses are customary prerequisites for computing courses, which most frequently involve learning to program in BASIC. As a result, female and minority students are far less likely to gain access to computers in school. The IBM Program promoted equal access to computing by focusing on personal computers as tools for all students in many subject areas. The data collected during the program suggest that the donated computers were used by female and minority students in the same proportion as these groups were represented in the U.S. secondary school population.

A fourth important aspect of the IBM Program was the creation of a centralized computer laboratory in each participating school. Strong encouragement was given to each school to keep the 15 PCs together in one location. We believed that creating a centralized laboratory that could be used by many different teachers for their courses would increase the benefit to students. The laboratory was meant to be defined as public territory with equal access to all. Furthermore, the laboratory was designed to encourage use by classes, for it was equipped with 15 PCs—thus classes of 30 could be accommodated, with two students sharing each computer. We had hoped that the laboratory would also lessen the probability that one teacher or department might commandeer the microcomputers for its own exclusive use.

In practice, the labs were heavily used by classes of students, however, a number of schools reported "turf" fights that occurred among department heads and teachers of computer programming and other subject areas. A teacher's ability to offer a semester-long computer-based course and the availability of commercially published curriculum materials often influenced the use of the laboratory.

Both IBM and ETS wanted to encourage the use of the donated hardware and software by *students*. We did not want the PCs to be removed from the laboratory by administrators or teachers, no matter how worthy the cause. Because the object of the donation was student use, the central laboratory was crucial to that purpose. Feedback received from teachers and administrators during the site visits revealed strong support for the concept of the laboratory.

A fifth feature of the IBM Program unique in computer-education programs, was the network support structure. We were certain that supplying hardware, software, and teacher training would not be enough, initially, to ensure optimal use of the donation. Rather, we expected that most schools would, in the beginning, have difficulty in using the PCs and would need further resources. It became clear during the course of the 1983-1984 school year that our concern had been justified.

However, by selecting schools in close geographic proximity to one another and by forming them into local networks with a central coordinating agency experienced in computer uses in education, we provided an opportunity for schools to draw upon additional sources of support as they incorporated the donation into their own organizational structures. The network furnished a central source of information for dealing with problems, and perhaps more importantly, it supplied cohorts of peers with whom teachers, administrators, and students might confer.

A sixth aspect of the program design, one that proved to be a key element, was the "layered" training provided to the faculty and staff of the TTIs, the high school teachers and administrators, and the secondary school students themselves. ETS provided the training for the TTIs; they in turn offered instruction to the high school staff who subsequently used the microcomputers with their students. As documented in chapter 7, the TTI staff gave favorable reviews to the ETS training, and the numbers of high school teachers, administrators, and students who received training and were using computers increased noticeably. Some recommendations for effective training strategies derived from our experience with this program are discussed.

The final distinctive feature of the IBM Program was its establishment of an extensive telecommunications network linking ETS, IBM and all the secondary schools and TTI's. Through the generosity of Hayes Microcomputer Products, Inc., Source Telecomputing Corporation, and Tymnet, Inc., each institution in the program received the requisite hardware, software, and free connect time for participation in an electronic mail and computer-conferencing system, and to use the many databases on the Source for instructional purposes. Admittedly, not all TTIs and high schools took advantage of these opportunities. Nevertheless, students and teachers in many of the schools did use the utility's databases and did engage in regular communication with other program participants and nonprogram subscribers, including those from foreign countries.

In sum, these characteristics made the IBM Program unique and created what we believe to be a major innovation in secondary school use of microcomputer technology. These experiences should prove valuable to other schools as they attempt to use educational technology in the years ahead.

RECOMMENDATIONS

The IBM Secondary School Computer Education Program was designed as a model program for others to learn from and build upon. In the previous section we discussed the key factors in the program's success. We now make the following recommendations on the basis of our experience in administering the IBM program and our work with other schools in the U.S. and abroad. We hope that these recommendations assist educators to design and implement exemplary computer-education programs.

Program Design

Develop a Written Plan for Integrating the Computer into the Learning Process. The outcome of the planning process should be a written plan that describes short-range and long-range goals, anticipated costs, and implementation timetables for instructional computing in the school or district. The plan should be responsive to the school's goals and include specific recommendations concerning curriculum development, staff assignments and training, software evaluation, hardware acquisition, site preparation, acquisition of consumable materials, equipment maintenance, ongoing professional development, and program evaluation. Provisions should also be made for regular, periodic review and updating of the planning documents.

Make a Multi-Year Commitment to Establishing a Comprehensive Program. Plan on committing substantial resources to making the program an integral part of the school for a minimum of 3 years. In most cases, it will take at least that long for a significant number of teachers to become comfortable using computers and for computing to become an integral part of the curriculum.

Use a Shared Planning Approach to Ensure a Broad Base of Participation and Support. In particular, involve the key administrator in the program's design, planning, and implementation. The goal setting and planning process should involve district admnistrators, building principals, department heads, teachers, school board members, and community representatives. It may also be useful to involve external consultants such as futurists, computer specialists, and leaders in computer education when developing goals and implementation plans.

The active participation and commitment of the building principal and district superintendent will be critical to the success of computer education programs. Any effort to establish a program, no matter how thoughtful and determined, will be severely hampered without the strong support of key administrators.

Teach All Students to Use Microcomputers as Tools to Facilitate Learning in Many Subject Areas and in Extracurricular Activities. Students should have an opportunity to develop competence in using computers by using word processors to improve their writing; using database programs to collect, classify, search, sort, and analyze data; accessing on-line databases and information utilities over telephone lines; developing and using computer models and simulations; controlling and monitoring laboratory experiments; and using the sound and graphics capabilities of computers to express themselves in the arts.

Ensure That Computing Programs Do Not Reinforce Economic, Racial, or Gender Disparities. Secondary school computing courses typically serve a narrow population of above-average students. Make a conscious effort to prevent this narrow focus by: (a) not linking computers exclusively to the math department; (b) eliminating unnecessary restrictive prerequisites; and (c) making computer use a requirement for all students.

Recognize That Using Computers in the Instructional Process Will Create Additional Work for Teachers. Although computers can be "productivity tools" in educational administration, their use in instruction will require more teacher preparation and support than traditional modes of classroom instruction. Educators in the participating schools in the IBM program identified this extra effort as one of the biggest single problems that they encountered. To prepare to use computers in the classroom, teachers will need a substantial amount of time to learn about computers, develop or adapt curriculum, prepare lessons, schedule facilities, manage the learning environment, and evaluate student performance. Don't underestimate the importance of this recommendation.

Teach Computer Programming Effectively So That Students Can Construct Their Own Tools. In many computer-programming courses, students rarely learn more than the mechanics of a programming language. Knowledge of such mechanics, however, will not prepare them to write a useful program. Students should learn how to define problems, plan strategies, write structured code, test solutions, evaluate the results, and refine their solutions. Select machine-specific and language-specific curriculum materials that will help students achieve this goal by utilizing the computer's color, graphics, and sound capabilities as a vehicle for instruction.

Establish a Computer Coordinator Position. If the school's computers "belong to everybody," then nobody has a vested interest in managing and caring for this valuable resource. The coordination and management of a school's computing resources should be the responsibility of a paid staff member who is given the authority to manage the resources according to the school's goals and objectives so that maximum educational use can be realized. The computer coordinator should be compensated, be given a decreased teaching load, or be relieved of other duties.

Hardware and Software

Establish a Central Computer Laboratory. Rather than distribute microcomputers throughout the school, concentrate a critical mass of computer hardware and software in a central laboratory at the secondary level. This centralization will enable teachers to work effectively with class-size groups of students. Strive for no more than a 2:1 ratio of students to computers. Provide adequate supervision for the lab and make it available to students, faculty, and community members before, during and after school hours.

In schools that have already established one or more computing laboratories, distribute additional microcomputers in the library, science labs, art rooms, learning-interest centers, or department offices.

Choose Computer Hardware That Will Permit Expansion. Select hardware that can be upgraded easily. New software products frequently will require larger memory capacity and additional peripheral devices. Anticipate the need to add disk drives, modems, graphics tablets, light pens, plotters, and a letter quality printer.

Select Reliable Hardware That Will Stand Up in a School Environment. Anticipate a heavy pattern of use by students, teachers, and community members. Select hardware on the basis of the manufacturer's track record for producing reliable equipment and providing timely and cost-effective service. A service center located far from the school will be of little value; look for a way to service the equipment locally.

Allow Sufficient Time for Site Preparation, Delivery and Installation of Computer Systems. Don't underestimate the costs, amount of time, and technical expertise needed to get a whole lab up and running. Anticipate "slippage" in delivery dates, and make sure that new computers are unpacked and used extensively during the initial warranty period so that problems are identified and repairs can be made at no cost.

Choose Software That Is Easy-To-Learn and Use. Select products that permit students and teachers to become comfortable and productive using the computer in the least time possible while still providing the features users will need. Occasional users will find it frustrating to use many of the more sophisticated packages.

Make Sure That Software and Hardware Are Compatible. Don't take anything for granted. Determine the requirements for the minimum amount of memory, operating system, disk drives, cables, and peripheral devices and find out if the hardware and software will work together. Interfacing microcomputers with printers and plotters can be particularly problematic; whenever possible, make this interface the vendor's responsibility.

Encourage and Assist Staff to Purchase Their Own Personal Computers. Negotiate vendor contracts that permit school employees to purchase computer hardware and software at educational and quantity discount prices. If possible, provide staff with low-interest loans to purchase their own computers.

Professional Development

Place a High Priority on Computer Education for Teachers and Administrators. The overall success of the program will depend on the enthusiasm, support, and ability of educators to learn about and realize the potential of computing in schools. The first step must be for educators to develop comfort and competence in using computers. Recognize that this will require a lot of time and resources to make plans to provide both.

Focus Staff Development on Integrating Computers Into the Instructional Process. Design activities and group projects that complement traditional school courses, extracurricular programs, and curriculum materials. Teachers should also be encouraged to design and teach courses preparing students for careers in the information age.

Select Training Personnel Who Have Adequate Knowledge, Experience, and an Ability to Communicate With Teachers. Instuctors must know about computing, about using computers in education, and furthermore, must demonstrate respect for the teachers they will instruct. Choose instructors who are well organized, directive, evaluative, and also creative and flexible. Finally, teacher trainers should have a good sense of humor and skill in communicating technical topics.

Compensate Staff and Make Participation Voluntary. Staff attending programs should be there by their own choice. Free choice ensures an adequate level of motivation and commitment to the program. Staff should be compensated for their time in accordance with school or district policy on professional development.

Ensure That Staff Members' First Experiences in Using Computers Are Successful, Relevant, and Nontrivial. Introduce staff to computing through easy-to-use applications software; it is best to begin with word processing. Avoid extensive discussion of related, but not directly applicable, computer topics. Don't start by teaching computer programming or operating system commands.

8. SUMMARY AND RECOMMENDATIONS 137

Reduce Lectures and Start Staff Using Computers as Quickly As Possible. Introduce applications packages quickly. Then assign a nontrivial task or a simple project that requires using the applications software. Finally, assign complex group projects that require participants to design, select, and integrate the use of different applications. A good example would be to publish a newspaper, requiring the use of word processing, a spelling checker, electronic thesaurus, graphics packages, and database manager.

Plan Inservice Schedules to Provide Extensive Hands-On Time and to Reduce Distractions and Inconvenience. Make certain that staff can have ample time and access to computers during and between formal presentations. Avoid "one-shot" training programs. Plan for continuing contact or on-going support in one form or another. Provide sufficient classroom space and enough computer hardware so all staff can have access. Use computers that are similar to the equipment available in school, as well as appropriate software.

Identify Participants' Expertise and Encourage Peer Teaching. Design activities that encourage interaction among staff and sharing of information. Help to create patterns of communication that will continue after formal training is over.

Ensure That Staff Have Access to Computers for Extended Periods After School Hours. Staff should be encouraged to take computers home in the evenings, during weekends, and over school vacations. Acquire a sufficient number of systems so that they can be made available to staff on a rotating basis. Purchase carrying cases to reduce wear and tear on systems, and make certain that the school's insurance policy covers damage or theft to the equipment while it is off the school's premises.

Don't Forget the Administrators. Be certain that the professional development program includes administrators as well as teaching staff. In particular, building principals and district administrators will need to: (a) develop realistic expectations of how computers can and should be used; and (b) recognize the extent of organizational resources required to implement and sustain quality computer-education programs.

Support Activities

Establish a Regional Network to Provide Essential Support Services. One major lesson that we learned in the process of administering the IBM program was the value of the support network. We strongly recommend that schools embarking on computer education programs create support networks for themselves to identify existing resources for technical assistance, software evaluation, hardware maintenance, and curriculum materials. The member schools may also choose to aggregate purchases of hardware, software, and consumable materials to realize quantity discounts.

Perhaps a local teacher-training institution might be persuaded to play the role of network coordinator. Colleges and universities having education programs may be interested in establishing relationships with nearby schools. You may also want to contact schools in your area to create a network of schools using similar hardware and software.

Conduct Regular Meetings with Other Schools. Plan to have regular meetings with faculty and administrators of other schools to share information and strategies. Joint projects on curriculum revision of other program features should be initiated. Computer fairs or competitions might be sponsored jointly. Regular visits to other schools should be made by teachers. If collaborations between schools are not possible, encourage teacher-user groups within your school. Provide space and time for meetings and a small budget for speakers.

Provide Incentives and Resources for Educators to Belong to National and Local Organizations. Make it possible for teachers and administrators to attend computer-education conferences and seminars sponsored by established organizations. Conferences can be invaluable in making contacts with other professionals. Professional journals of the leading organizations are a rich source of up-to-date information in a quickly changing field.

Financial Considerations

Budget for Much More Than Just the Cost of the Hardware. Budget adequate amounts for site preparation, staff development, curriculum development, ongoing support services, instructional materials, maintenance, security, additional software, and consumable materials. In projecting cost estimates for all these items, consider how the computers will be used, what the extent of teacher involvement will be, and where the machines will be located. All these factors will affect program costs.

Obtain Broad Support for All Aspects of the Program. In seeking support of computer-education programs, schools should attempt to develop partnerships with institutions in their region: local industry, institutions of higher education, community agencies, and parent organizations. All these institutions are potential sources of contributions, matching funds, equipment, software, technical expertise, and staff time to support the program.

8. SUMMARY AND RECOMMENDATIONS 139

Offer Computer-Education Programs for the Community As a Service and a Source of Revenue. Schools should become more responsive to the needs of adults in their communities. With a population that is rapidly advancing in age, continuing education is growing in importance. Get the community directly involved in the schools by using the schools' microcomputers after hours and during the summer to offer courses as part of adult and continuing education programs. Schools that have been engaging in such activities report that adult school programs have been directly responsible for community support of school budgets and bond issues.

Think Entrepreneurially. Charge adult school participants appropriate lab fees so that schools can generate revenue to subsidize the cost of hardware maintenance and the acquisition of new software. The same computer facilities can also be used for teaching specialized business applications to employees of business and industry. Teachers will welcome the opportunity to augment their income by serving as faculty members for these after-school courses.

Know the Funding Sources. Make certain that at least one person in the school or district keeps informed about new state and federal programs, vendor programs, contests and competitions, foundation grants, and other sources that may provide resources or funding for computer education programs.

SUMMARY

In this final chapter we highlighted the most significant elements of the IBM Secondary School Computer Education Program and presented a series of recommendations for schools to consider when implementing and maintaining their own computer-education activities. It is our hope that the lessons we learned will be useful to our colleagues in high schools nationwide as they adopt this potentially revolutionary technology to serve students.

Epilogue

Two programs were subsequently initiated by IBM in the area of computer education. The first program began in the fall of 1983 when representatives of the Americas/Far East division of the IBM World Trade Corporation expressed interest in conducting similar programs in foreign countries. ETS staff were consulted and site visits to U.S. TTIs and secondary schools were made. Based on what had already been learned about the U.S. secondary school program, ETS staff made specific recommendations concerning the design of programs abroad.

In May 1984, ETS staff conducted an intensive computer education institute in Sydney, Australia; again, the program focused on the use of computers as tools for secondary school teachers and students. The 2-week program, similar to the previous year's training offered by the TTI staff in Princeton, was attended by faculty of teacher-training institutes and officials of government education agencies from Australia, Canada, New Zealand, and Malaysia. In these countries, local IBM offices had decided to establish donation programs (with appropriate modifications to reflect regional conditions) in order to promote effective school use of microcomputers.

ETS designed and conducted the training of the Teacher Education Institute (TEI) staff, each country then making arrangements for organizing and maintaining its own programs. The extent to which the four countries adapted the original features of the U.S. program varied considerably. The Australian program employed many aspects of the U.S. program. A significant departure was that IBM Australia, Ltd. decided to make a 3-year commitment of continuing support to the participating TEIs and high schools.

During the Sydney training, ETS staff worked with Professor Terry Cannings of Pepperdine University, one of the Los Angeles area TTI's trainers in the U.S. program. Cannings, an Australian and an internationally recognized expert in computer education, was able to establish a rapport with the trainees that was most helpful. His contributions were substantive.

The training included the use of computers linked to telecommunications networks to access on-line databases and electronic mail systems. As a result, there now exists the possibility of creating an international telecommunications network among secondary school students and teachers.

The second program began in the spring of 1984 when IBM launched a second-year computer education program in the United States. This $12 million program, which ran through the 1984–1985 school year, was an extension of the program IBM conducted with ETS in the U.S. It was administered by the University of South Florida, one of the original Tampa area TTIs, and Bank Street College of Education, in New York City. This program included the 25 largest school districts in the U.S., with the exception of those in the three states that participated in the original effort. Superintendents chose as participants five intermediate or secondary schools in their districts and one local agency to serve as the network coordinator. All schools and agencies received from IBM hardware and software comparable in value to the donation in the first-year program. The layered training, network support, and telecommunications capability were also featured in the expanded program. IBM announced plans to document the second-year program and to make it widely available. Independent evaluations of both programs will be completed and published.

Thus, IBM has conducted two major computer education programs, which have already attracted national and international attention. These programs, with their emphasis on the computer as a tool and on teacher training, network support, and telecommunications are having a major impact on the introduction of computers into schools.

Indeed, Andrew Barbour (1984) reported a dramatic shift in educational computing in American classrooms. In *Electronic Learning* magazine's Fourth Annual Survey of the 50 state departments of education, he states that:

1. Educators are shifting computer education away from programming and toward the use of computer applications such as word processing, spreadsheets, and data base management.
2. Emphasis is increasingly being placed on the integration of computers in the curriculum, rather than confining computer use and instruction to a single programming or computer-awareness course.
3. In order to foster this new vision of an applications and curriculum-based computer literacy, both in-service and pre-service, teacher-training programs are on the rise.

We hope that the IBM program has contributed to this trend toward the integration of computers as tools in education.

Appendix A: Microcomputer Laboratory Design and Usage Suggestions[1]

Design Philosophies

In a teaching laboratory, worktables can be arranged in rows facing the teacher in a conventional classroom manner. A disadvantage in this layout is that student interaction during open (non-lesson) periods can be very disrupting.

In a working lab, worktables are arranged in U or L shapes to allow group interaction yet permit a degree of privacy.

In another setting, an "island" arrangement with two PCs on each side of a table worked well. This configuration encourages students on opposing sides of the table to share information.

Space Requirements

There should be a minimum of 5 linear feet of workspace per machine (preferably 6 ft) and a depth of 2 ½ ft. Factors that will affect these dimensions are machines with peripherals and security devices that need additional space. Plan to leave access to the rear of the machines for maintenance and configuration enhancements. Special considerations must be given to left-handed students. Two feet of work space at one side of the machine is included in this arrangement.

---

[1] Adapted from J. DeGilio. (Undated). *Microcomputer laboratory design and usage suggestions.* Unpublished manuscript. Used by permission.

Worktables

Fixed tables are preferable to movable ones because of wiring, security, and stability of the equipment. The optimum height for the tables for adult operators has been found to be 26 in. For younger students, adjustments should be made. Table material should be sturdy and durable to withstand the equipment weight and the students' pressure.

Screen Height

Beginners will be constantly looking from the screen to the keyboard so that the distance from the keyboard to the bottom of the screen should be about 1 or 2 in. Experienced users will appreciate a greater distance, about 4 in.

Noise Insulation

Many of the peripherals, especially the printers, have a high noise level. Installation of dividers or booths for the computers with printers will help reduce the noise level. For optimal utility and budget considerations, booths should accommodate two students.

Static Electricity

In large computer systems, static electricity is a problem of some concern, but in a microcomputer lab there are typically few problems. Thick pile carpeting or any nylon carpeting should be avoided, and the humidity level in the room should be kept at 50% or higher. Anti-static carpets and aerosol sprays are commercially available if the conditions warrant; however, a solution of one part water and three parts fabric softener will suffice to use in spray dispensor for static electricity control on the carpets.

Air Conditioning and Heat

Temperature in the lab should not exceed the range of 55-90°. If in non-classroom hours, the temperature drops or exceeds this range, allow at least 1 hour at 70° before attempting to use the equipment. Excessive humidity and heat will damage paper supplies and diskettes if exposure is prolonged.

Lighting

Direct sunlight can cause significant glare problems for screen viewing, especially with color monitors. Window shades should be installed to control this. General lighting should be well diffused (e.g. fluorescent lights) to avoid monitor glare.

Power Requirements

IBM PCs need approximately 500 watts of electricity; that includes the system unit, the monitor, and the printer. Four grounded outlets should be provided for each single PC station. Power surge protectors are a must in areas where power fluctuations are frequent and/or wide. A surge protector can be purchased for $35 to $80 from any computer store. These devices will not provide security from power dips. Voltage regulators cost about $400 and should be used to protect against major power fluctuations. One voltage regulator per line should be sufficient while the surge protectors can be used on one or two PCs.

Wires and Switches

Wiring and outlets should be at the table level to avoid the common problem of kicking the plugs from the outlets. The abrupt and unexpected power drop will definitely result in unretrievable data and could damage the machine. Do not use extension cords and power strips. Master switches can be used to control all of the power to the PCs, but system units should be turned off before cutting the power to the line supporting the lab equipment. There is little danger to the equipment if the master switch is cut and machines are on, as long as no one is in the middle of a disk write. Monitors should not be turned off between classes to avoid temperature fluctuations, which wears out the CRT. It would be preferred to turn the brightness control down to a dim image rather than turn them off. Intense brightness settings can damage a CRT if left on for long periods of time.

Care and Feeding of the Lab

Keep the room clean. Do not have a chalk blackboard in the room at all. Chalk is one of the leading causes of damage to diskettes and drives. In one high school recently visited, the building computer coordinator complained that they had persistent diskette drive failures unlike any other high school seen. When the classroom where the micros were located was inspected, the reason was evident. There was a thick layer of chalk dust over all of the equipment.

Monitor screens should be cleaned frequently with damp cloth and a mild solution of soap and water. Dust levels should be kept to an absolute minimum since accumulation of dust will increase the temperature within the machine and result in equipment failure. This problem is especially acute in printers where paper and ribbon dust require vacuuming regularly.

A carbon dioxide or halogen fire extinguisher should be available and in good working order.

No eating, drinking, or smoking should ever be allowed within the lab.

Care of Diskettes

Upon installation of the operating system to the software packages, always make a working copy (if the license allows) for everyday use and place the master diskette in a safe, dry, dark place. Backing up diskettes applies also to data files that have value as well.

When creating program or data diskettes, label the contents immediately. Do not write directly on the diskettes, fill out the labels, then affix them to the diskettes.

Be careful to avoid opening diskette drive doors while the red drive light is on.

The diskette should be handled by the plastic case. Never touch the exposed portions of the diskette material. The oil and salt content on your skin can result in diskette read errors.

Again, chalk dust, smoke, cigarette ash, any liquids, food, playful little people and animals all have been known to wreck a diskette.

Invest in good quality diskettes. Cheap diskettes typically cause more problems and lost teacher-time than they save in the beginning. Good quality diskettes can last for many years and can be reused with confidence.

Extreme temperatures will destroy diskettes. Do not store them in places where they will be exposed to direct sunlight.

There is only one way to insert a diskette into a drive; that is, gently and in the proper direction with the right side up. Every student working in the lab should know the procedure by heart.

Diskettes should be kept in their sleeves, in the proper boxes or cases with identifiable labels.

Keep diskettes away from magnetic fields such as those found near television sets, electronic motors, fans, typewriters, loudspeakers, and airport x-ray equipment.

Appendix B: Publications About the IBM Secondary School Computer Education Program

Bacon, G. (1984, July). A PC for the teacher. *PC World, 2*(7), 292-299.

Bennett, R. (1984, November). Teachers reach out and touch with PCs. *PC Magazine, 3,*(22), 335-337.

Berger, H. (1984, April). An IBM first for secondary schools. *PC Magazine,* 165-170.

Cline, H. F., & Anderson, J. (1984, Summer/Fall). A program for teaching the teachers. *Perspectives in Computing, 4*(2/3), 39-46.

Levy, J. (1984, January). Each one teach one. *Softalk for the IBM Personal Computer, 2,* 88-96.

Scarino, M. C. (1984, February). Student aid from IBM and Apple. *PC Magazine,* 134-139.

Schneiderman, M. (1984, October). Making the case for innovation. *Popular Computing,* 88-95.

Wagner, W. J. (1983, Autumn). Giving with a plan: the training component of the IBM Secondary Education Program. *Computers and Teacher Education, 10*(4), 42-53.

Watt, D. (1983, December). The IBM connection. *Popular Computing,* 75-78.

Watt, D. (1984, October). Practical teaching tool. *Popular Computing, 3*(12), 54-59.

References

Anderson, E. S. (undated). *TTI coordinator's summary report: IBM Secondary School Program, 1983-84.* San Jose, CA: San Jose State University.

Barbour, A. (1984, October). Computing in America's classrooms, 1984: The new computer literacy emerges. *Electronic Learning 4*(2), 39-44, 100.

Bennett, R. E. (1984). Evaluating microcomputer programs. In R. E. Bennett & C. A. Maher (Eds.), *Microcomputers and exceptional children* (pp. 83-90). New York: Haworth.

Bennett, R. E. (Ed.). (in press). *Planning and evaluating computer education programs.* Columbus, OH: Charles E. Merrill.

Bernard, H. C. (1984). *IBM Personal Computer lab: Coral Gables Senior High School.* Coral Gables, FL: Coral Gables Senior High School.

Bloom, B. S., Hastings, J. T., & Madaus, G. F. (1971). *Handbook on formative and summative evaluation of student learning.* New York: McGraw-Hill.

Boyer, E. (1983). *High school: A report on secondary education in America.* New York: Harper & Row.

Campbell, P. B., & Gulardo, S. (1984). Computers in education: A question of access. *Computers in the Schools, 1,* 57-65.

Center for the Social Organization of Schools. (1983a, April). *School uses of microcomputers, 1,* 7. Baltimore: Johns Hopkins University.

Center for the Social Organization of Schools. (1983b, June). *School uses of microcomputers, 2,* 2-5. Baltimore: Johns Hopkins University.

Center for the Social Organization of Schools. (1983c, October). *School uses of microcomputers, 3,* 2-4. Baltimore: Johns Hopkins University.

Center for the Social Organization of Schools. (1984, June). *School uses of microcomputers, 5,* 4-6. Baltimore: Johns Hopkins University.

Haggart, S. (1978). *The resource approach to the analysis of educational project costs.* Washington, DC: U.S. Government Printing Office.

Jamison, D., Suppes, P., & Butler, C. (1970). Estimated cost of computer-assisted instruction for compensatory education in urban areas. *Educational Technology, 10,* 49-57.

Kiresuk, T., Lund, S., & Schultz, S. (1981). Service delivery and evaluation from the consumer's point of view. In S. Ball (Ed.), *New directions for program evaluation: Assessing and interpreting outcomes* (pp. 57-70). San Francisco: Jossey-Bass.

REFERENCES

Levin, H. M. (1975). Cost effectiveness in evaluation research. In M. Guttentag & E. Struenig (Eds.), *Handbook of evaluation research: Vol. 2* (pp. 89–122). Beverly Hills, CA: Sage.

Levin, H. M. (1983). *Cost-effectiveness: A primer. (New perspectives in evaluation: Vol. 4).* Beverly Hills, CA: Sage.

Lockheed, M. E., & Frakt, S. B. (1984, April). Sex equity: Increasing girls' use of computers. *The Computing Teacher, 11* (9), 16–18.

Miura, I., & Hess, R. D. (1983, August). *Sex differences in computer access, interest, and usage.* Paper presented at the annual convention of the American Psychological Association, Anaheim, CA.

National Commission on Excellence in Education. (1983, April). *A nation at risk: The imperative for educational reform.* Washington, DC: U.S. Department of Education.

National Science Board Commission on Precollege Education in Mathematics, Science, and Technology. (1983, September). *Educating Americans for the 21st century.* Washington, DC: National Science Foundation.

Ragosta, M., Holland, P., & Jamison, D. (1982, April). *Computer-assisted instruction and compensatory education: The ETS/LAUSD study* (Final report to the U.S. National Institute of Education). Princeton, NJ: Educational Testing Service.

Scriven, M. (1974). Evaluation perspectives and procedures. In W. J. Popham (Ed.), *Evaluation in education: Current applications* (pp. 1–94). Berkeley, CA: McCutchan.

Shavelson, R. J., & Winkler, J. D. (1982, June). *Can implementation of computers be justified on cost-effectiveness grounds* (P-6781). Santa Monica, CA: Rand.

Shavelson, R. J., Winkler, J. D., Stasz, C., Feibel, W., Robyn, A. E., & Shaha, S. (1984). *"Successful" teachers' patterns of microcomputer-based mathematics and science instruction* (N-2170-NIE/RC). Santa Monica, CA: Rand.

Stecher, B. (1984a). Improving computer inservice training for teachers. *AEDS Journal, 18*(2). Washington, DC: Association for Educational Data Systems.

Stecher, B. (1984b). *Training teachers to use computers: A case study of the summer training component of the IBM Secondary School Computer Education Program (RR 84-25).* Princeton, NJ: Educational Testing Service.

Task Force on Education for Economic Growth. (1983, June). *Action for excellence: A comprehensive plan to imporve our nation's schools.* Denver, CO: Education Commission of the States.

Twentieth Century Fund Task Force on Federal Elementary and Secondary Education Policy. (1983). *Making the grade.* New York: Twentieth Century Fund.

U.S. Bureau of the Census. (1984). *Statistical abstract of the United States: 1984.* Washington, DC: U.S. Government Printing Office.

Wolf, M. (1978). Social validity: The case for subjective measurement *or* how applied behavior analysis is finding its heart. *Journal of Applied Behavior Analysis, 11,* 203–214.

Author Index

A,B,C

Anderson, E. S., 81, 82
Barbour, A., 142
Bennett, R. E., 111
Bernard, H. C., 77
Bloom, B. S., 111–112
Boyer, E., 2
Butler, C., 108
Campbell, P. B., 6, 122

D,F,G

DeGilio, J., 141
Frakt, S. B., 6, 122
Feibel, W., 118
Gulardo, S., 6, 122

H,J,K

Haggart, S., 89
Hastings, J. T., 111–112
Hess, R. D., 6, 122
Holland, P., 108
Jamison, D., 108
Kiresuk, T., 124

L,M

Levin, H. M., 89, 90, 108
Lockheed, M. E., 6, 122
Lund, S., 124
Madaus, G. F., 111–112
Miura, I., 6, 122

R,S

Ragosta, M., 108
Robyn, A. E., 118
Schultz, S., 124
Scriven, M., 120
Shavelson, R. J., 108, 118
Shaha, S., 118
Stasz, C., 118
Stecher, B., 56, 68
Suppes, P., 108

W

Winkler, J. D., 108, 118
Wolf, M., 124

Subject Index

A

Access to computers, 113-114, 122-123, 131, 134, 137
ACS Communications Support (program), 34
Activities
　extracurricular, 6, 71, 114
　summer institute, 56-58
　support, 137-138
Administration
　professional development for, 136, 137
　support of, 52-56, 67-68, 74, 76, 94, 98-99, 126, 127
Adult education, 71-72, 77, 108, 124, 139
Adventures in Math (program), 35
Affiliation, school, 24
Affluence, level of, 15, 24-25, 134
Aggregated costs, 99-101
Air conditioning, 96, 105, 144
Alpha Software Corp., 36
Ambach, Gordon M., 12
American High School (Florida), 77
Apple Computer Corporation, 2, 3, 130
Apple IIe, 3
Applications software, 51-52, 72, 75, 130-131
Arithmetic Games (program), 34, 36
Atlanta meeting, 75-76

B

Background, program, 1-3
Bank Street College of Education, 142
Barry University, 12-13, 17, 18, 46
BASIC language, 6, 55, 70, 115
Benefits, 108-109
Bennett, Randy, 41
Binghamton, New York area, 10, 13, 14, 18, 20
Bitter, Gary, 41
Boards of Cooperative Educational Services (BOCES), 12-17, 18, 20, 46
BPI General Accounting (program), 36
Brand of microcomputer, costs and, 105-106
Branscombe, Lewis, 2
Broome-Tioga BOCES, 13, 14, 18, 20
Brown, Edmund G., Jr., 12
Budget, 100, 138. *See also* Costs

C

CAI, 69, 70, 75, 103, 104
California
　inservice training in, 12, 71
　secondary school networks in, 19-21
　special state funds in, 107
　TTI institutes in, 10, 13
Cannings, Terry, 141-142
CBASIC Compiler (program), 36
Chalk, damage from, 145
Classroom space, 95
Class size, 28
Clubs, computer, 71
Cognitive effects, 121-122

153

154   SUBJECT INDEX

Color monitor, 106
Commitment, administration, 53-56. *See also* Support
Commitment duration, 75, 126, 127, 133
Communications, 64-67, 83. *See also* Telecomputing
Community, adult education for, 71-72, 77, 108, 124, 139
Community, affluence of, 15, 24-25
Compatibility, hardware-software, 135-136
Compensation, teacher, 22, 56, 67-68, 74, 97, 136
Computer Access Corporation, 36
Computer assisted instruction (CAI), 69, 70, 75, 103, 104
Computer coordinator position, 134
Computer Discovery (program), 34, 35, 36
Computer laboratories
   design and maintenance of, 28, 143-146
   location of, 105, 113-114, 131, 135
   security, 30-31, 72-73, 94, 96, 105
   telephones in, 66
   TTI, 48, 59
   wiring for, 96, 105, 145
Computer(s). *See also* Hardware
   access, 113-114, 122-123, 131, 134, 137
   clubs, 71
   costs of, 93, 94, 103-104
   installation, 84, 135
   languages, 6, 42, 55, 70, 115
   social implications of, 109
   use of
      across subject-matter areas, 81, 115-117, 118, 133-134
      contexts of, 6, 69-72, 103
      extent of, 72, 104
      increase in, 114
      program cost and, 103-104
      TTI reports on, 76-81
Conferences, 40, 138. *See also* Meetings
Consultation, 83, 94, 97. *See also* Network support
Consumer reaction, 124-127
Coordination, costs/resources of, 98
Coordinator, computer, 134
Coral Gables High School (Florida), 77
"Core" software packages, 32-33
Costs, 87-109
   aggregated, 99-101
   analysis procedures, 89-91
   cost-benefit analysis, 108-109
   defining, 89
   distribution of costs/resources, 91-99
   illustrative dialogue about, 88-89
   preliminary projections compared with, 101
   program characteristics and, 102-106
   resources needed, 101-102
   sources of funds, 106-108, 139
Creativity of teacher-trainers, 60
Cross Clues (program), 34, 35
Curriculum, teacher agreement over, 123
Curriculum-based projects, 52, 54-55
Cybertronics International Corp., 36

D

dBase II (program), 36
Delta Drawing (program), 36, 55, 125
Design, computer lab, 28, 143-145
Design, program, 4-7, 10, 11, 17, 28, 133-134
Diskette Librarian (program), 34, 35
Diskettes, care of, 146
Distribution of costs/resources, 91-99
District resources, 107
Donations, 1, 14, 48, 107, 129-130. *See also* Hardware; Software
DOS 2.1 (program), 35
Duration of program, 75, 126, 127, 133
Dust, damage from, 145

E

EasyWriter (program), 32, 33, 51, 54, 71, 125
Education, trends in, 2, 3
Educational Testing Service (ETS)
   encouragement of IBM program, 3
   network support, 63-81
      communications, 64-67
      midyear meetings, 73-76
      reports, 76-81
      site visits, 67-73, 112
   Sydney, Australia program, 141-142
   software selection and, 33-36
   teacher-trainer training, 40-46, 132
Effects, related, 120-124
Electronic Learning (magazine), 142
Electronic mail system, 65-66
Enrollments, 24, 80
Equipment. *See* Hardware
ETS. *See* Educational Testing Service (ETS)
Evaluation, 44-46, 61, 124-127
Expansion, hardware, 135
Extent of use, 72, 104
Extracurricular activities, 6, 71, 114

SUBJECT INDEX   155

F

Facilities, 58–59, 94, 95–96, 102. *See also* Computer laboratories
File Command (program), 35
Financial considerations, 74, 126, 133, 138–139. *See also* Costs
Financial crisis in Los Angeles, 16
Flexibility of teacher-trainers, 60
Florida. *See also* Barry University; Polk County School District; University of South Florida
  adult education program, 72
  inservice training in, 12, 71
  secondary school networks, 16, 17–20
  TTI sites in, 10
Florida Atlantic University, 12–13, 16, 17, 18, 50, 83
Format, TTI instructional, 41–44
Fortran, 70
Free Enterprise (program), 36
Funds, sources of, 106–108, 139
Furniture, 59, 94, 95, 106

G

Gender, computer access by, 122–123, 131, 134
Generic applications software, 51–52, 75, 130–131
Geographic locations, 4–5, 9–10, 11
Goals, program, 6, 7, 37–38, 42–43, 57, 111–120
Goodson, Bobbie, 41

H

Hands-on practice, 57, 137
Hardware
  access to, 113–114
  components, 28–30
  costs/resources of, 93, 94
  installation, 84, 135
  maintenance and security, 30–31, 72–73, 93, 94, 105
  reactions to, 125, 126
  recommendations for, 135–136
  selection, 27–31, 37–38
  at summer institutes, 58
  telecommunications, 64–66
  for training teacher-trainers, 44, 45
  TTI goals and objectives for, 43

Hardware Maintenance and Service Manual, 32, 33
Hayes Microcomputer Products, Inc., 29, 36, 64, 132
Heat, 144
Henry Chauncey Conference Center, 44, 46
Home Budget (program), 34

I

IBM BASIC Compiler (program), 34, 35
IBM Cobol Compiler (program), 34
IBM Corporation
  announcement of program, 11
  donations, 1, 14, 48
  duration of involvement, 75, 126, 127, 133
  initiation of program, 1
  introduction of PC, 2–3
  network support, 83–84
IBM Fortran Compiler (program), 34, 35
IBM Pascal Compiler (program), 34, 35
IBM Secondary School Computer Education Program. *See* Program
IBM World Trade Corporation, 141
Impact. *See under* Program
Implementation, planning for, 57
Inservice training, 12, 71, 77–80, 98, 102
Installation, 84, 135
Institutional support, 52–56, 67–68, 74, 76, 94, 98–99, 126, 127
Institutions, effects on, 123–124
Instructional process, integrating computers into, 136
Instructor (program), 125
Instructors, 41, 47. *See also* Teacher-trainers; Teachers
Insulation, noise, 144
Interaction, social, 52, 57, 137

J, K

Jobs, Steve, 3
Johns Hopkins University, 131
Journals, professional, 138
Karel the Robot, 36
Kershaw, Roger, 41
"Kids Can't Wait" program, 3, 130
Knowledge, teacher-trainers, 59, 136
KoalaPad TouchTablet, 19, 36
Koala Technologies Corporation, 29, 36

SUBJECT INDEX

L

Laboratories. *See* Computer laboratories
Languages, computer, 6, 42, 55, 70, 115
"Layered training," 5-6, 132
Learning, computers as tools to promote, 6, 69-70, 103
Learning DOS 2.0 (program), 35
Learning to Program in BASIC (program), 34, 35
Lessons, structured, 57
Lighting, 59, 144
Locations, geographic, 4-5, 9-10, 11
Logistical support, 59
Logo (program), 35, 36
Los Angeles, California area, 10, 16
Los Angeles TECC, 13, 19, 20-21
Los Angeles Unified School District (LAUSD), 16, 18, 20
Lotus, 37
Luehrmann, Arthur, 41

M

Macchiarola, Frank J., 16
Macro Assembler (program), 34, 35
Maintenance, computer lab, 145-146
Maintenance, hardware, 30-31, 73, 93, 94
Market Data Research database, 15, 24
Mass media, attention of, 11
Materials, costs/resources of, 95, 99
McGraw-Hill Book Company, 36
Meetings, 73-76, 81-83, 138
Miami, Florida area, 12-13, 16-18, 46, 50, 83
Miccosukee Indian School, 28
Microcomputer industry, success of, 2-3
MicroIllustrator (program), 29
Micropro, 37
Microsoft, 37
Midyear meetings, 73-76
Monitor, color, 106
Monster Math (program), 35
Multiplan (program), 32-34, 36, 55, 70, 125
Multi-year commitment, 133

N

National Center for Education Statistics (NCES), 24
National Science Board, 2, 4
National Science Foundation (NSF), 2
National Survey of School Uses of Microcomputers, 121-122, 131
Negotiations, school selection, 21-22
Networks, 1, 5, 17-21, 68
Network support, 63-85
  costs/resources of, 94, 97
  ETS, 63-81
    communications, 64-67
    midyear meetings, 73-76
    reports, 76-81
    site visits, 67-73, 112
  IBM, 83-84
  recommendations for, 137-138
  school staff reaction to, 127
  structure, 131-132
  TTI, 42, 81-83, 119-120
Newsletters, program, 67, 83
Newspaper, school, 71
New York City area, 10, 13, 16, 18, 20, 50, 52
New York State
  adult education programs, 72
  inservice training in, 12, 71
  secondary school networks, 18-19, 20
  TTI sites in, 10
Noise insulation, 144
NSF, 2

O, P

Off-site and on-site consultation, 83
On-site inservice training, 98
Operating system, 43
Parents, involvement of, 81, 107
Pascal, 70
PC Learning (newsletter), 67
Peach Text (program), 34
Peer teaching, 137
Pepperdine University, 13, 19, 21, 50, 53
Peripheral devices, 43, 93
Personal Editor (program), 34, 35
Personnel, costs/resources of, 94-95, 97-99. *See also* Teachers; Teacher-trainers
pfs program series, 32, 34, 36, 37, 51, 54-55, 70, 71, 125
PL/1 Compiler (program), 36
Planning, 57, 70, 98, 123-124, 133
Poirot, James, 41
Polk County School District, 13, 14, 20, 46, 53, 73
Poughkeepsie, New York area, 10, 13, 18, 20, 52, 81, 83
Power requirements, 145
Principals, 53-56, 126-127. *See also* Administration
Private donations, 107

SUBJECT INDEX

Private Tutor (program), 34, 35
Professional development, 80, 104, 136–137.
   See also Inservice training
Professional Editor (program), 34, 35
Professional journals, 138
Professionals, teachers as, 60
Professional services, costs/resources of, 94, 96–97
Program
  background, 1–3
  characteristics, cost and, 102–106
  design, 4–7, 10, 11, 17, 28, 133–134
  duration of, 75, 126, 127, 133
  goals, 6, 7, 37–38, 42–43, 57, 111–120
  guidelines, 22
  impact, 111–128
    consumer reaction, 124–127
    goal attainment and, 111–120
    related effects, 120–124
  newsletter, 67, 83
  planning, 57, 98, 123–124, 133
  significance of, 129–132
  for teacher-trainer training, 41
Programming, 6, 33, 81, 104, 115–117, 134
Projections, cost, 101
Projects, curriculum-based, 52, 54–55
Proportional representation, 14–15, 24–25, 130
Publications, computer education, 147
Putnam/Northern Westchester BOCES, 13, 18, 20

Q, R

Queens College, 13, 18, 20, 50, 52
Question (program), 54, 125
Race, computer access by, 122–123, 131, 134
Radio Shack, 2
Rapport, teacher-student, 123
Reactions, consumer, 124–127
Recommendations, 132–139
Related effects, 120–124
Reliability of hardware, 135
Remodeling, 94, 95–96, 102, 105
Repair, hardware, 93, 94
Reports to ETS, 76–81
Representation, proportional, 14–15, 24–25, 130
Resources
  categories, 92, 101–102
  hidden, 99
  identifying and valuing, 90–91
  institutional, 52–56

  sources of funds, 106–108, 139
  use, distribution of, 91–99
Respect for teachers, 60
Rural schools, representation of, 24

S

San Jose, California, selection of, 10
San Jose midyear meeting, 73–75, 76
San Jose State University, 13, 20, 21, 80–81, 83
Santa Clara Teacher Education and Computer Center, 13, 20, 21, 83
Satisfaction, consumer, 124–127
Schneiderman, Martin, 41
School affiliation, 24
School newspaper, 71
Science education, 2
Science Research Assoc., 36
Screen height, 144
Secondary schools. *See also* Costs
  definition of, 4
  equipment donated to, 1, 107
  ETS site visits to, 69–73, 112
  location of, 4–5
  selection of, 14–25
  staff reactions, 126–127
  statistics on, 23–25
Security, hardware, 30–31, 72–73, 94, 96, 105
Selection
  of hardware, 27–31, 37–38
  of participants, 9–25
    secondary schools, 14–25
    of teacher-trainers, 40
    TTIs, 9–14
  of software, 27, 31–38
Shared planning approach, 133
Significance of program, 129–132
Sites, training, 10, 44, 48
Site visits, ETS, 67–73, 112
Snooper Troops 1 and 2 (programs), 34, 35
Social effects, 121, 122
Social interaction, importance of, 52, 57, 137
Socioeconomic status, 15, 24–25, 134
Software
  access to, 113–114
  availability of, 4, 6
  -based assignments, 57–58
  costs, 93–95, 102, 103–104, 106
  generic applications, 51–52, 75, 130–131
  reactions to, 125, 126
  recommendations for, 135–136
  selection, 27, 31–38

158 SUBJECT INDEX

at summer institutes, 58-59
telecommunications, 64-66
for training teacher-trainers, 44, 45
TTI goals and objectives for, 42
usage of, 74-75
Software Publishing Corp., 36
SourceMail, 65-66, 68
Source Telecomputing Corporation, 29, 37, 64-66, 75, 132
Space requirements, 95, 143
Special-interest groups of teachers, 51
Spinnaker Software, 36
Spreadsheets, 70, 75
Stark, Peter, 3
State funds, special, 107
States n' Caps (program), 35
Static electricity, 144
Statistics on participating schools, 23-25
Structured lessons, 57
Student organizations, 71
Students, effects on, 121-123
Subject-matter areas, 48, 49, 81, 115-117, 118, 133-134
Suburban schools, representation of, 24
Summer institutes for teachers, 46-61
common characteristics of best, 56-61
costs/resources of, 98
site visits during, 68
training at, 46-56
Supplemental staff, costs/resources of, 95, 99
Supplies, costs/resources of, 95, 99
Support. *See also* Network support
activities, 137-138
financial, 74, 126, 138
institutional-administrative, 52-56, 67-68, 74, 76, 94, 98-99, 126, 127
logistical, 59
relationships, increasing, 119-120
Switches, computer, 143
Sydney, Australia, program in, 141-142

T

Talley, Susan, 41
Tandy Corporation, 130
Teacher Education and Computer Centers (TEECs), 12, 13, 15-16, 19, 20-21
Teacher Education Institute, 141
Teachers
activity, categories of, 97-98

compensation, 22, 56, 67-68, 74, 97, 136
effects on, 123
reactions of, 126-127
respect for, 60
special-interest groups of, 51
time needed by, 134
training, 46-56, 117-119, 126, 136
Teacher Support Group, 47
Teacher-trainers, 40-46, 59-61, 136
Teacher-training institutes (TTIs)
common characteristics of best, 56-61
ETS and
communications with, 64, 65-67
midyear meetings with, 73-76
reports to, 76-81
site visits to, 67-69
goals and objectives, 42-43
hardware for, 14, 29, 48, 58-59
network coordination by, 1, 5
network support, 42, 81-83, 119-120
reactions to, 125-126, 127
selection of, 9-14
selection of schools and, 15, 17
sites of, 10, 48
software selection for, 32
staff training. *See* Training
Teaching methods, 47, 50-51, 137
TECCs, 12, 13, 15-16, 19, 20-21
Technical Reference Manual, 32, 33
Technical representatives, IBM, 83-84
Telecomputing, 29, 42, 64-66, 75, 93, 94, 132, 142
Telephone contact, ETS, 64
Telephones, 65-66, 96
Time problems, 73-74, 134
Tioga Central High School (New York), 77-80
Trainers. *See* Teacher-trainers
Training, 39-61
common characteristics of best, 56-61
inservice, 12, 71, 77-80, 98, 102
"layered," 5-6, 132
reactions to, 125-26, 127
resources needed, 102, 103
sites, 10, 44, 48
of teachers, 46-56, 117-119, 126, 136
of teacher-trainers, 40-46
Travel costs/resources, 95, 99
Trends, 2-3
TTIs. *See* Teacher-training institutes (TTIs)
Tymnet, Inc., 29, 37, 64, 132
Typing Tutor (program), 32, 33

U,V

U.S. House of Representatives, 3
UCSD Fortran Compiler (program), 34, 35
USCD Pascal Compiler (program), 34, 35
USCD p-system Fortran (program), 34, 35
USCD p-system Pascal (program), 34, 35
University of South Florida, 13, 17, 18, 47, 51, 142
Urban schools, representation of, 24
Value of resources, determining, 90-91
Vassar College, 13, 18, 20, 52, 81, 83
VisiCalc (program), 32-34, 36, 55, 70
Visicorp, 37

W

Warranty service, 31
Westchester County, selection of, 10, 13
Westchester/Putnam BOCES, 46
Wiring, computer lab, 96, 105, 145
Word processing, 70, 74-75, 81, 115
Wordskills levels 3-6 (programs), 35
Wordwhiz (program), 35
Workshops, 83
Worktables, 144